Rapid Writing in 6 Days

RAPID
Writing in 6 Days

The Quick-and-Easy Program
to Master Faster Writing

Ben E. Johnson, Ph.D.

A PERIGEE BOOK

This book is dedicated to

Alice A. Perry
William Perry
Iris Joy Watters
Robert Watters

Whose love, sacrifice, and generosity will not be forgotten.

A Perigee Book
Published by The Berkley Publishing Group
200 Madison Avenue
New York, NY 10016

Book design by Irving Perkins Associates

Cover design by Bob Silverman, Inc.

First Perigee edition: September 1994

Published simultaneously in Canada.

Library of Congress Cataloging-in-Publication Data

Johnson, Ben E.
    Rapid writing in six days : the quick-and-easy program to master
faster writing / Ben E. Johnson.
        p.   cm.
    ISBN 0-399-52132-1
    1. Shorthand—Alphabet.   I. Title.   II. Title: Rapid writing in 6
days.
Z56.2.A45J64   1994
653'.15—dc20   93-43993
                                                                         CIP

Printed in the United States of America

10   9   8   7   6   5   4   3   2   1

CONTENTS

INTRODUCTION

I know what I know and I write it.

—Octavio Paz

While teaching at a college in the suburbs of Chicago over twenty years ago, I developed and taught a note-taking and rapid writing course for my students in order to help them keep up with their lecture-intensive classes. Each semester, I received scores of thank-you notes from grateful students who said their new rapid writing skills were instrumental in helping them master classroom lectures. Later, I started teaching these same rapid writing skills to others, high school students and their parents, local businessmen, office workers, other teachers, all who had heard from their children—my students—that there was a way to listen and take notes more effectively while also writing faster, and they too wanted to learn how to do this. In the more than two decades since then, that system of rapid writing, taught back then and now described in this book, has helped thousands of people, students and professionals, to at least double their writing speeds, while many have tripled. I have put that rapid writing training in this book.

In many ways this book is actually much more like the rapid writing classes I taught than like a book. You see, this is not just another book to be *read*, it is a book to be *worked in and completed*. There is "homework"—exercises, work sheets, and progress tests—and admonitions from me to hang in there and keep trying.

Unlike most books, which provide the reader with all the information needed to be entertained or informed on a relatively passive level, this book requires reading *and* doing if it is to be helpful; it is designed to be worked in, written in, used as a workbook. You will read it, piece by piece, then you will write in it. You will do exercises in it that will help you acquire the skills of rapid writing that you are reading about. Without the "work" part of this workbook, you might end up understanding the practical things it teaches, but you still wouldn't be a faster writer: you would know how to rapid-write, but you wouldn't be able to do it.

So you're going to have to try everything in this book if you're going to be a successful rapid writer. But I assure you, when you do try, you'll be rewarded. Who knows—you might even get your name in *The Guinness Book of World Records* for breaking speed writing records. It could happen. When that happens, call me. I'll buy you dinner to celebrate. And just so you'll know which records you have to break, here are the current world's records for fast writing.

Current Speed Writing Records
(*according to* The Guinness Book of World Records, 1993)

1. The highest recorded writing speeds ever attained under championship conditions in the United States are 300 words per minute (99.64 percent accuracy) for five minutes and 350 words per minute (99.72 percent accuracy) for two minutes, by Nathan Behrin in tests conducted in New York in December 1922.

2. The European writing speed record is currently held by Mr. Arnold Bradley of Walsall, Great Britain, who on November 9, 1920, had the unique distinction of writing at 309 words per minute in a five-minute test—and without making an error.

There, now you have something to shoot for. Good luck—and let's get started.

STEP 1

Start Now: This Is Going to Be Much Easier Than You Think

The Moving Finger writes; and, having writ,
Moves on: nor all your Piety nor Wit
Shall lure it back to cancel half a Line,
Nor all your Tears wash out a Word of it.

—The Rubáiyát of Omar Khayyám,
translated by EDWARD FITZGERALD

Few people are able to speak *articulately* at a sustained speed above 300 words a minute.

Periodically, most of us find ourselves in situations where we are envious of secretaries. In fact, even secretaries sometimes find themselves envious of those highly skilled, highly trained secretaries and stenographers who are proficient in shorthand and who can take dictation, copy down conversations, or take notes at speeds of up to 150 words per minute. And what's even more impressive is that these same people can actually *read* what they have written at those outrageous speeds. Those funny-looking almost-letters seem to make sense to them. Wow! What we wouldn't give for that ability.

Unfortunately, we know we're not willing to pay the price to acquire those skills. We would have to return to school, taking shorthand courses at a local college or business school for at least a year (but probably for two years) before we could hope to be anywhere close to proficient at transcribing what we hear or read into all those funny, seemingly meaningless symbols and squiggles. We don't have the time or the money to do that. On top of this, we would also have to do hundreds of hours of practicing before we could really even attempt to use what we were learning—and we probably still wouldn't be able to write very fast. Add to all of this the depressing fact that shorthand classes aren't very interesting. What all this means is that we have several reasons for not learning traditional shorthand, and this leaves us with a problem.

The Problem: "I Can't Write Fast Enough"

No matter who you are, you're probably expected at times to take notes quickly and accurately, and you know that you just can't write fast enough. Perhaps you are self-employed and are struggling in your business to keep up with all the new products and price changes that are reported to you daily by telephone. Perhaps you are working in an office and frequently are called upon to take notes at department meetings; perhaps you are a secretary or clerk who is called upon to take dictation, and even though you were not hired to take dictation, you find yourself stumbling along writing everything out longhand, feeling inadequate and somehow embarrassed because you are certain that the person dictating to you doesn't recall that taking dictation isn't part of your job description. Or maybe you are enrolled in college classes and the instructors all seem to lecture at ninety miles per hour, while you can take down what they are saying at the rate of only twenty miles per hour. You always seem to be playing catchup in your note taking, losing major sections of the lecture in the process and never having time to think about what the professor is saying because you're too busy writing. You know you're missing out, but you don't know what to do about it.

The Solution: Learn Rapid Writing

Fortunately there is a relatively painless solution: *you can learn an alphabet shorthand and at least double your writing speed!* You can learn an alphabet-based shorthand system, a system of rapid writing that uses recognizable letters, not funny dots and squiggles. And what's more, you can learn every-thing you need to know to acquire this rapid writing system in just six days. That's right. Not six years, or six months, not even six weeks—just six days. This means that you'll be able to write twice as much in the same amount of time, so that you have more listening and thinking time—something that was missing before.

Break the Old Lazy Writing Patterns

With few exceptions our writing training in school has been focused on what to say rather than on writing, and that's understandable. But, by the very nature of how we were taught to write, we have developed some inefficient writing patterns. Some of us are still very aware of our elementary school training and spend much too much time forming perfectly shaped letters. If we have taken a calligraphy course at some time, our letters and words now may have all those attractive embellishments we like to see in greeting cards, which are not good for quick writing and note taking.

And then there are those of us who went the other direction: we didn't work very hard in elementary school on our penmanship, we never think about our sloppy writing now, and we don't really care how illegible our writing is to other people. But we're going to have to break these old patterns of slow, embellished, or illegible writing if we're going to learn to use rapid writing.

Learning to rapid-write in just six days is more than possible for everyone who reads this book. If you are willing to invest your effort, your time, and your determination, you will be pleasantly surprised by this time next week.

Steps to Rapid Writing

In beginning to use this book, it's important that you know where you're going and how you're going to get there. Throughout this book you'll be instructed to employ a variety of new (to you) methods for building faster writing. You're probably wondering just how you are going to achieve this miracle of faster, more efficient writing and note taking in just six days. Let me put your mind at ease. There is no magic, no tricks, just some simple new writing techniques for you to master one day at a time. You will learn:

1. A simplified alphabet
2. Fifty basic symbols and wordsigns that will double your writing speed
3. A system for omitting letters when you write rapidly that will further increase your writing speed
4. A system for quickly abbreviating and writing the beginnings and endings of words that will have you writing faster yet
5. A simplified system for taking notes that enhances your rapid writing skills

As you continue reading you will begin by *simplifying* the forms of some letters (*ι* for *t*, for example) to create a slightly revamped alphabet. Next will come *substituting* certain easily remembered symbols for fifty common words that you write all the time (such as \ for *the*). If you do nothing else but this, you'll be able to write twice as fast from this point on. From there, you'll learn to trim words further through the *omitting* of unnecessary letters (like *akmdl* for *accommodate*). *Abbreviating* the beginnings, endings, and key parts of words will come next (*n. Y.* for *New York* and *ad.* for *advertisement*). All of this will be followed with an easily learned system of note taking that is enhanced by rapid writing.

You Must Invest a Little Time and Effort

Despite the immediate appeal of a shortcut like rapid writing for those in both the business and academic communities, the term *rapid writing* can be misleading. Rapid writing is not something for nothing. In order to gain speed in writing for future use, a certain small personal sacrifice of time must be made now. A little time now and the determination to make use of the resources available to you in this book are really all you need to be on your way to doubling your writing speed. Fortunately (and this is where this book is unique among "speed writing" instruction), you will be surprised at how small that sacrifice of personal time actually is.

Avoid Supersonic Scribbling

One thing you cannot sacrifice while gaining writing speed, however, is readability. As you will soon discover, supersonic scribbling alone or using a self-made, self-taught shorthand system full of inconsistencies won't save you time if later you can't decipher what you wrote. Consistency and uniformity—in essence, readability—ought to be a major goal of your learning and practicing rapid writing.

Practice, Practice, Practice

This book is designed to simplify your learning of rapid writing skills. The most strategic method to learn this material is simple, short, regular drilling; therefore, there are many brief and practical exercises in this book for each of the six days that most people take to complete the reading and instruction. Use the drills. They will help you learn quickly. Practice what you are learning whenever you get a few minutes, and try to do so frequently. From now on, every time you write something for yourself, use what you have learned and rapid-write. Soon the techniques of rapid writing will become spontaneous.

Guidelines for Mastering Rapid Writing

Once you get started learning how to rapid-write, you will want to keep six important guidelines in mind:

1. Read and Learn Only One Section of This Book at a Time

This book is divided into six parts. Your goal is to read—and complete—one part each day for the next six days. You are in the first part right now, getting an overview and understanding of what's ahead. Each of the six sections is self-contained and has its own practice drills to reinforce your learning. Because this book is developmental—each new lesson is based on the preceding lesson—you are asked to faithfully complete each section before you move on to the next chapter. But don't move on until you have read, understood, and practiced all the drills that are assigned in the section you are in. You must resist the urge to skip about in this book and "sample" the instructions that look interesting to you.

Once the material covered in this first lesson is understood and practiced, what follows in the next five sections will seem easier.

2. Don't Wait to Use Your New Skills

Obviously you can't learn all that this course teaches in the first day, but you can learn something of value to apply immediately to writing and note taking. Use these new skills right along with longhand on everything you write. Gradually, over six days, you will add more and more rapid writing techniques until you are writing more rapid writing wordsigns than longhand words.

3. Start Sounding Everything Out

This is very important. You will be taught to write words not as you know they are spelled, but *as they sound*. Get in the habit of saying each word in the drills aloud as you write it. (There will be several exceptions to this system of writing words as they sound, but the reasons for these exceptions will be obvious.) You may want to limit your speaking aloud as you write to times when you are alone.

4. Don't Worry About Spelling

One of the most difficult things for you to train yourself to do when you learn to rapid-write is to separate the "correct" spelling in your rapid writing from the actual correct spelling. You will rapid-write everything "incorrectly," using a system of abbreviations and shortened words in order to write faster. Consequently, none of your rapid writing wordsigns will be spelled "correctly." You will still be able to read your wordsigns quickly, and you will know what they mean, but they will look funny—like the attempted spellings of a kindergartner. Just don't worry about how things are spelled when you are rapid-writing.

5. At First, Don't Worry About Speed

Initially, the most important thing in learning this rapid writing system is accuracy, not speed. For most people that is hard to accept, because what they really want to learn is faster writing. But if you thoroughly learn the basics of each section and then take time to practice carefully, concentrating on accuracy, speed will increase naturally as you go along. Later on, there are many exercises for building speed.

6. Use What Works

Many techniques are suggested in this book for improving your writing speed and note-taking proficiency. Be certain to try them all when they are presented. Some readers will find that everything suggested helps in improving their rapid writing ability, while others will find that only selected techniques make a significant difference. Remember, you won't know what works until you try. After you're all finished with the lessons, forget the things which don't work very well for you, and focus your practice efforts on those points that you have found to be *very* helpful. There are more than enough helpful things in this book to double your writing speed even if you discard a few techniques that aren't helpful.

FIND OUT HOW FAST YOU NOW WRITE

It's time now to find out what your present writing rate is for comparison purposes so that periodically you can test yourself, compare your new rate with this beginning rate, and find out how quickly your writing speed is increasing.

Printed below is Abraham Lincoln's Gettysburg Address. In the space under each line below, copy the words to the Address as quickly as you can. Please write directly in this book. This is a workbook and it is designed for you to write in. Time yourself by writing your beginning time on the line provided. When you finish copying the lines, record your finishing time on the line provided at the end of the Address.

Beginning time _____

Fourscore and seven years ago our fathers brought forth on this continent a

new nation, conceived in liberty, and dedicated to the proposition that all men

are created equal.

Now we are engaged in a great civil war, testing whether that nation,

or any nation so conceived and so dedicated, can long endure. We are

met on a great battlefield of that war. We have come to dedicate a portion

of that field as a final resting place for those who here gave their lives

that that nation might live. It is altogether fitting and proper that we should

do this.

But in a larger sense, we cannot dedicate—we cannot consecrate—we

cannot hallow—this ground. The brave men, living and dead, who struggled

here, have consecrated it far above our poor power to add or detract.

The world will little note nor long remember what we say here, but it can

never forget what they did here. It is for us, the living, rather, to be

dedicated here to the unfinished work which they who fought here have

thus far so nobly advanced. It is rather for us to be here dedicated to the

great task remaining before us—that from these honored dead we take in-

creased devotion to that cause for which they gave the last full measure of

devotion; that we here highly resolve that these dead shall not have died in vain; that this nation, under God, shall have a new birth of freedom; and that

government of the people, by the people, for the people, shall not perish

from the earth.

Ending time ⎯⎯⎯⎯⎯

Subtract your beginning time from your ending time to determine how fast you were writing. Record here ⎯⎯⎯⎯ how many minutes you spent writing. Indicate the number of minutes in terms of the closest quarter of a minute. For example, 6 minutes and 18 seconds would be rounded off and written as 6.25, while 5 minutes and 30 seconds would be written 5.5. Now that you have determined how many minutes you spent writing, divide 267, which is the total number of words in the Gettysburg Address, by your time spent writing. This will let you know how many words per minute you were writing. Record your words-per-minute rate below.

Words per minute (wpm) ⎯⎯⎯⎯⎯

How Did You Do?

Now that you know how fast you can copy material and you have an idea of what your present writing rate is, compare it to the rates below.

Longhand writing rates:

Below average	20–30 wpm
Average	35–50 wpm
Above average	50–60 wpm

Speaking rates:

Average college professor	100–125 wpm
Fast-talking professor	125–175 wpm
Fastest public speech on record	336 wpm°

(°Surprisingly, a portion of a speech by President John F. Kennedy in December 1961.)

One thing is clear from these figures. Without learning to rapid-write you will not be able to record two-thirds of what you hear.

Now It Is Time to Really Get Started

This ends Step 1. See, that wasn't bad at all. In fact, if you aren't worn out yet—and you shouldn't be—why not get started with Step 2, where the actual rapid writing instruction begins.

STEP 2

Take a New Look at an Old Alphabet

The right to write badly was the privilege we widely use.

—Isaac Babel

Sean Shannon, a Canadian residing in Oxford, Great Britain, recited Hamlet's soliloquy "To be or not to be" (259 words) in a time of 24 seconds—equivalent to 647.5 words per minute—on British Broadcasting Corporation's *Radio Oxford* on October 26, 1990.

All of us take the letters of our alphabet for granted. They are familiar to us, they are not something that we ever talk about; they're just there and we employ them routinely. But not any longer. In this chapter you're going to learn a second alphabet composed of the same letters as your original alphabet, but written more efficiently. By the time you finish this book, you will still have and use your usual alphabet for "normal" writing, but you will also have a simplified alphabet designed for faster writing.

The Alphabet As It Should Be Written

As you know, there are twenty-six letters in the alphabet, all of which are very familiar to you. To learn rapid writing you will not have to learn a new alphabet, nor will you have to learn a system of squiggles and dots. You will only have to learn a slightly revised alphabet. The chief difference between the old alphabet and this new one is that all unnecessary strokes, curves, loops, and embellishments are left off in writing the letters of this new alphabet. Since our penmanship patterns are just that, established patterns, this streamlining of our alphabet is a bit difficult to accomplish without some serious effort and practice to break out of those old patterns. The exercises are designed to assist you in eliminating old penmanship patterns while developing your new rapid writing alphabet patterns.

Removing all of these "extra" parts of the alphabet is done for speed and clarity. Since we are in the business of shaving seconds off our writing, it only makes sense that we remove whatever extra strokes we have added to our penmanship over the years. At the same time, we want to make sure that none of our letters is mistaken for another letter—which for many of us happens frequently with our writing now.

Shown below is an alphabet geared to swift, flowing writing. Look at the letters carefully. Notice how they are formed. Learn them.

Notice the Differences

Look carefully at this "new" alphabet. Look at which characters have loops and which ones don't. Also, what makes the t different? Do you dot the i and the j? Where are the capital letters?

The Missing Letter C

Notice also that this alphabet is not very different from the alphabet you learned in grammar school, except for one thing: something's missing. This alphabet does not contain the letter C. Think about the way letters sound. There is no C sound! The letter C has two sounds: the sound of K if it is a hard sound, and the sound of the letter *S* if it is a soft sound. For example, the word *combat* begins with a hard *C*, the sound of *K*. The word *city*, however, begins with the soft *C* sound, the sound of *S*.

Since we are going to rapid-write words the way they sound, we will use either *K* or *S* when we need a *C* sound. You will see shortly that this makes it much easier to read our rapid writing notes.

Why Bother?

But wait a minute, you may be thinking, why bother simplifying my penmanship? A reasonable question. Why should you bother to practice, study, and learn an alphabet so similar to the one you learned as a child? The answer is obvious if you will look at something you have written recently in haste. If you are like most people, your writing style has changed over the years, and most likely the change has been toward illegibility.

Perhaps you tend to disconnect letters, like *this*, or perhaps you make beautiful calligraphy, the way some MEDIEVAL SCRIBES WROTE . Some people stop writing altogether and begin to *print*. And some people get just plain *sloppy* and *illegible*. All of these practices may be all right in themselves, but they certainly work against your rapid writing proficiency. You need to perfect your rapid writing alphabet, and that comes only through practice. So, let's do some practicing.

ALPHABET DRILL 1

As you can see, all unnecessary lines and loops have been eliminated from the design of each letter. Your goal is to be able to write in this compacted style automatically. Write each letter in the alphabet as many times as space permits.

a

b

d

l

f

g

k

l

j

k

l

m

n

o

p

q

r

s

t

u

v

w

x

y

z

ALPHABET DRILL 2

Now write the letters of this alphabet as connected letters of one word. Fill the entire page and don't raise your pen at all.

Repeat Drill 2 again, but before you start, examine your writing carefully in Drill 1. Are you forming each letter carefully as it should be formed, or are you just writing the way you always do? Practice forming each letter of the alphabet carefully. Don't worry about speed at this point.

Learn to Write Unusual Letter Combinations

In the English language, some letters are never written next to one another because they can't be pronounced together. In rapid writing, you will find that any letter can be written next to any other. You will need to get in the habit of writing every letter in combination with every other letter without thinking about it, and without a feeling of resistance when you write.

ALPHABET DRILL 3

Now practice writing letters in combinations. Some of the combinations below may seem difficult to write because you are being asked to write some combinations that you have never put together before. Write each group of letters three times in order to continue working on overcoming any bad habits of penmanship and to learn to write easily letters in unusual combinations.

qd   rf

pe   yh

pv   ik

wm   pm

zg   bv

ws   cx

za   vr

dc   ny

gb   im

jm   hg

lo   fd

ju   qe

gt   et

de   yu

aq   mn

xw   hy

lj   sx

ux   fv

io   hn

ed   kl

tg   ki

uj   hy

ol   fr

nb   sw

vc   zq

xz   ce

bt   ds

mu   wr

jh   ry

gf   ui

ALPHABET DRILL 4

Now combine four letters into a nonsense word. Write each word twice.
Remember, this is a penmanship exercise, so don't get sloppy. Your goal is to
develop a streamlined alphabet with no extra curves, lines, loops, or bends.

plok   iuyj

ytgh   ytrg

vgft   oplu

xdrf   refh

qrum   cliu

fjrd   plzv

tdfx   jkld

asht   xnbm

mbys   ygcb

iphg   jkfg

yhvb   jghk

ujkl   pbbt

rtgf   lhty

mhrw   znbb

shkm   lkyp

phkj	bntr
sfhg	aliy
zxxz	vnyt
iujm	oifg
nbmh	koih
cfre	lhdw
aszw	xuye
cdxg	xwsf
mkjy	wsqr
cbzo	mnyt

xvcb   ssfd

pyts   rvrr

xfhy   bnyy

wqty   ddgt

cbfw   wtrr

tbvd   qynf

tphx   yhkj

rtyu   jklh

Did you notice how few vowels you were writing for the last several lines of "words"? The reason for this will soon become clear.

Now go back and check the exercises you've done so far to see if your *b*'s look like *l*'s. They shouldn't. Does your *f* look like this? *f*   There should be no dots on any *i*'s or *j*'s. Is your *t* crossed? It shouldn't be. Do all your *l*'s have loops, or do they look like a new rapid writing alphabet *t*? Any *f, g, j, q, y*, and *z* should have loops. Examine what you have written.

Skill-Building Practice Will Speed You Up

You are now coming to that portion of this book where you'll be expected to do a lot of practicing. Remember, a little time and commitment at this point will bring you big rewards.

Write, Don't Print

Did you catch yourself *printing* the letters occasionally while you were doing these drills? Resist that temptation to print, because it slows you down when you're rapid-writing.

ALPHABET DRILL 5

Now try writing the following real words using your streamlined alphabet. Write each word at least two times on each line. Remember, at this time you are not going for speed, you are going for a perfected penmanship.

at   spool

glass   hand

from   boot

see   tooting

let   partridge

telling   quit

question	frame
book	desk
took	xylophone
just	floor
dinosaur	disk
light	pope
triumph	mrs
flower	supervisor
glasses	football
wall	triumph
stand	share

leather	leaving
restaurant	try
turbo	fight
yellow	tone
sift	tomb
trust	zoology
friendly	boat
bowl	hole
running	tribble
maybe	madam
together	quantity

window   president

antler   mr

swift   payment

bark   alligator

boss   television

dish   glasses

pony   fried

plantor   zeta

louvre   verbatim

Now go back and write each word as quickly as you can without falling back into any old penmanship habits. Remember, your b's should not look like h's. Are all your letters connected to one another? Check to see that you put loops in the right letters. If you still find yourself using your old penmanship, practice writing these words correctly before you continue.

Let's Start Speeding Things Up

Once you're able to write the rapid writing alphabet fairly smoothly and consistently, it's time to start putting a bit of an emphasis on writing faster. Gradually through the course of this book you'll be pushed to go faster. Now is one of those times. Don't forget though that your first priority is developing and improving your penmanship—then your speed.

ALPHABET DRILL 6

Write each of the following words just once *as rapidly as you can, using your new alphabet penmanship. Record your beginning and finishing times and determine your writing speed. Repeat the exercise one more time, again timing yourself. Notice how much faster you can write when you're familiar with the words and the formation of the letters. That's why this book emphasizes practice. The more you practice, the faster you'll be able to rapid-write.*

1. Beginning time _____ Ending time _____ Total time _____

2. Beginning time _____ Ending time _____ Total time _____

desk   horn

dresser   glass

dart   window

gymnasium   typewriter

grass   mental

weather	port
belt	lamp
ladder	jaguar
invoice	memory
nesting	tragedy
harm	vault
pile	organ
sweet	door
gloves	picture
printer	sign

ginger	fight
flower	handle
treetop	sewing
orange	blanket
deadly	serial
piano	mouse
horse	flower
basketball	deforestation
deadline	mountain
sleigh	highpoint

Take a moment and glance back over your words. Did your penmanship get sloppy when you speeded up? Circle any letters that you did not form properly and practice writing them several times until you write them easily and naturally.

ALPHABET DRILL 7

Using the words below, repeat the procedure of Drill 6. Again time yourself as you write both times. There are the same number of words (50) in this exercise as in Drill 6. Is your transcription time speeding up?

1. Beginning time _____ Ending Time _____ Total time _____

2. Beginning time _____ Ending Time _____ Total time _____

roof	evening
automobile	lobster
train	oyster
airplane	shell
brief	whisper
heavens	skiing
morning	digest

fussbudget	expenses
beast	polish
story	perfume
spreadsheet	bulletin
elevator	dessert
using	puddle
rapidly	poodle
yourself	shed
time	trailer
writing	davenport
substitution	westerfield

refrigerator	quill
blanket	quite
pillow	alphabet
turtle	again
wherewithal	familiar
reset	important
annual	spent

Again, examine your penmanship after each writing of the words. Circle any letters that you formed improperly and practice writing those letters.

Proceed with Confidence

Once you're writing the new alphabet with confidence—and with some speed—you may proceed to a very important next step in learning to rapid-write: the substitution of special symbols or wordsigns for commonly used words.

STEP 3

Use Symbols or Wordsigns to Increase Your Writing Speed

True ease in writing comes from art, not chance,
As those move easiest who have learned to dance.

—ALEXANDER POPE

Steve Woodmore of Orpington, Great Britain, spoke 595 words in a time of 56.01 seconds, or 637.4 words per minute, on the ITV program *Motor Mouth* on September 22, 1990.

In order to employ an efficient system of rapid writing, you will have to have more rapid writing resources available than merely a streamlined alphabet.

One very effective rapid writing technique is to use a series of abstract symbols (sometimes called wordsigns because they stand for an entire word) whenever possible. These symbols are substituted when you write frequently used words or groups of words. This can be extremely effective because of the following facts:

Fact One:

Twenty-five percent of all written communication in the English language is made up of just ten words.

That's right. When we write, we use just ten words over and over again, so frequently in fact, that one of those ten words is used on the average every five words.

Fact Two:

Of these ten frequently used words, five compose 20 percent of all written communication.

Fact Three:

Two of these words make up 10 percent of all written communication.

The Ten Most Frequently Used Words

Obviously, if we can identify these commonly used words and create symbols or wordsigns that are much quicker to write than the words themselves, we can significantly increase our writing speed. Fortunately, we *can* identify these words. Listed on the following page are the ten most frequently used words, followed by the wordsigns we'll use as substitutes for the words when they are written. Take a few minutes to study these common words and their symbols.

Percentage of Use			Word	Wordsign
25%	20%	10%	1. the	\
			2. and	/
			3. of	f
			4. to	2
			5. I	ι
			6. a	.
			7. in	n
			8. that	u
			9. you	u
			10. for	4

Practice writing these wordsigns for a few moments before you read on. Use the space next to the wordsigns above to duplicate the wordsign for each word. As you write the wordsign for each word, repeat the word aloud. This will help you associate each wordsign with the proper word. Do it now.

Did you confuse the wordsigns for *the* (\ ) and *and* (/)? A handy way to remember which one is which is to keep in mind that the wordsign slants in the direction of the tallest letter in the word. The tallest letter in the word *and* is *d*, therefore the wordsign slants to the right, toward that letter. The tallest letter in the word *the* is toward the left side of the word, therefore the wordsign slants up to the left.

Notice that the strange-looking wordsign for *that* is actually composed of a crossed *t* and an uncrossed *t* joined together.

Each of these wordsigns can be written in less than half the time it takes to write out the whole word.

A Word About Doing the Skill-Building Drills

The following drills are designed to establish some patterns of thinking and writing. Do as many drills as necessary not only to learn how to rapid-write but also to feel that your learning is still being challenged. Once you feel you have the hang of it, stop drilling and start using your new skill.

WORDSIGN AND SYMBOL DRILL 1

Practice writing the wordsigns for the ten most commonly used words until you are able to write the proper wordsign for each word without having to stop and think about it. Write the wordsign as many times as you can on the same line as the word. Say the word aloud, or to yourself if you wish, each time you write it.

the

and

of

to

I

a

in

that

you

for

the

and

of

to

I

a

in

that

you

for

of

you

the

a

that

to

and

for

of

I

a

the

Make Use of Common Wordsigns You Already Know

At different times, all of us have learned a number of descriptive symbols—another name for wordsigns—used to save time in math class, chemistry, engineering, and at times on the job. These symbols do not have to be kept isolated from your everyday writing. They can be pulled out of their math or engineering context and used to save you time writing anything you want. Stir up your thinking. What symbols do you recall that can be pulled into your rapid writing arsenal? Remember these?

up	↑	over	⌢	greater than	>
down	↓	under	⌣	less than	<
check	✔	therefore	∴	approximate	~

What symbols can you remember, or invent, for words that you use often? List them below.

Now turn to the series of symbol drills that follow. See how long it takes before you know the new symbols thoroughly—or do you know them already?

WORDSIGN AND SYMBOL DRILL 2

Write the wordsign for each word. Skip any that you do not think of immediately.

1. the
2. of
3. I
4. in
5. you
6. the
7. and
8. of
9. to
10. I
11. up
12. therefore
13. the
14. greater than

15. less than
16. down
17. for
18. the
19. of
20. and
21. to
22. that
23. and
24. a
25. check
26. I
27. to
28. you

29. I	45. of
30. that	46. the
31. therefore	47. greater than
32. that	48. over
33. in	49. in
34. a	50. you
35. I	51. for
36. to	52. that
37. of	53. a
38. and	54. to
39. the	55. check
40. for	56. and
41. the	57. the
42. of	58. under
43. I	59. less than
44. in	60. therefore

Were there some wordsigns that you forgot? Check yourself by referring to the answers on the next page. Practice the symbols you invented for other words that you may use often.

Answers to Wordsign and Symbol Drill 2

1.	16.	31.	46.
2.	17.	32.	47.
3.	18.	33.	48.
4.	19.	34.	49.
5.	20.	35.	50.
6.	21.	36.	51.
7.	22.	37.	52.
8.	23.	38.	53.
9.	24.	39.	54.
10.	25.	40.	55.
11.	26.	41.	56.
12.	27.	42.	57.
13.	28.	43.	58.
14.	29.	44.	59.
15.	30.	45.	60.

WORDSIGN AND SYMBOL DRILL 3

Write the wordsign for each word and the word for each wordsign as fast as you can to test your speed and accuracy.

that		*t*
for		to
\		\
and		.
of		4
u		I
2		/
4		*f*
in		⟩
/		the
f		*ı*
.		*n*
t		∴
ı		*f*
in		⟨
u		that
and		you
of		2

⌣	＼
in	•
that	⌣
you	／
for	you
the	／
and	for
of	the
to	to
I	I
greater than	＼
up	⌣
down	↓
over	⌣
under	⊔
less than	✓
check	⊔
therefore	you
⌢	and
↑	for

Did writing the wordsigns come naturally? Check back to see if your wordsigns were accurate and well formed. Make sure you did not confuse the wordsigns for and and the. Did you notice how easy it was getting to read the wordsigns? You should be seeing the wordsigns ⊥, /, n, and ⨍, and reading them as that, and, in, and of. Practice makes the difference. Do all the drills.

WORDSIGN AND SYMBOL DRILL 4

Push a little bit more for speed as you do this drill. Write the wordsigns for the following words two or three times after each word as quickly as possible.

up	over
down	under
over	greater than
under	less than
greater than	check
less than	therefore
check	up
therefore	down
up	over
down	under
over	greater than
under	less than
greater than	check
less than	therefore
up	down

WORDSIGN AND SYMBOL DRILL 5

Using wordsigns, write the following nonsense phrases as often as space permits.

1. less than that

2. more than I

3. over you for that

4. therefore I for you

5. you check over

6. I check under

7. a greater than I

8. to check under that

9. the less than

10. a checkup over you for that

11. in that therefore

12. in you I check the greater than

13. you less than of I

14. that of you

15. you and I

Check back to see if your wordsigns were accurate and well formed. Select those that were not and practice them repeatedly.

WORDSIGN AND SYMBOL DRILL 6

Now start practicing your developing rapid writing skills with real phrases and sentences. In the space under each line, rewrite each sentence, remembering to use the wordsigns you have learned. When there is a word whose wordsign you do not know, write it out completely, but use your new alphabet to do so. Remember not to use a period at the end of the sentences. A period stands for the word a. *Check your answers on the next page.*

1. I thought that the hat would cost less than that.

2. He can always do more than I can.

3. I looked over you for that balloon I lost.

4. Therefore, I will have to vote for you.

5. You check over the room for inspection.

6. I always check under the tables for that.

7. He has a greater voice than I.

8. The officer wants you to check under that bench.

9. The two is less than the six.

10. You need a checkup for that cough.

11. You have less than two weeks to make up your work.

12. That was very kind of you.

Did you think to not end your sentences with a period? Leave a larger than normal space between sentences to indicate the end of one sentence and the beginning of the next sentence. Remember, in rapid writing a period stands for the word a.

Answers to Wordsign and Symbol Drill 6

1. *ι thought tt ＼ hat would kost < u*
2. *he kan always do ＞ ι kan*
3. *ι looked ⌒ u 4 tt balloon ι lost*
4. *∴, ι will have 2 vote 4 u*
5. *u ✓ ⌒ ＼ room 4 inspection .*
6. *ι always ✓ ⌣ ＼ tables 4 tt*
7. *he has · ＞ voise than ι*
8. *＼ offiser wants u 2 ✓ ⌣ tt bench*

9. \ 2 is < \ six

10. u need . ✓ ↑ 4 u kough

11. u have < 2 weeks 2 make ↑ your work

12. u was very kind f u

Notice that these sentences don't end with periods and don't have crossed *t*'s or dotted *i*'s.

WORDSIGN AND SYMBOL DRILL 7

Using the following words and phrases as a base, create your own wordsign sentences with them. See how few words other than wordsigns you can put in each sentence.

Note: *Frequently at this point in your learning rapid writing and in doing these drills you will have to write out words for which you have not yet learned a wordsign. In those cases write the word or words out in longhand, using your rapid writing alphabet.*

1. up and down

2. over and under

3. less than I

4. more than you

5. you check over

6. a checkup

7. you and I

8. the greater than

9. check under that

10. a greater than I

11. to you for that

12. that of you

Wordsign and Symbol Drill 8

This is a test of speed. Push yourself to write the wordsign for each word as quickly as possible. If you can't think of a wordsign immediately, skip it and move on. When you are finished, come back and see which wordsigns you didn't remember and which ones you wrote in a sloppy fashion.

the	to	in
and	I	that
of	a	you

for	I	you
and	a	in
of	in	that
to	I	you
I	a	for
of	in	the
to	that	and
I	you	of
a	for	to
in	the	I
that	and	a
you	of	that
for	to	you
the	a	for
and	in	the
to	that	

WORDSIGN AND SYMBOL DRILL 9

Now try some longer sentences. Write each sentence twice *using the wordsigns you now know. If you have not learned a wordsign for a word, write it out in longhand, using the rapid writing alphabet. Remember not to use the letter* c.

1. In spite of you and the others, I want to do that for you.

2. Since I am no longer staying here, you will have to go.

3. This is for me to know, and it will never reach your ears.

4. They took so many pieces of that cake there was none left.

5. You and I are in need of that car for a way to the store.

6. I am sure you will like that job if you get it.

7. For you to feel that way, makes me a bit sad.

8. You and I are always thinking of that great night.

Now create a sentence below using only wordsigns.

Double Your Writing Speed by Learning to Use Just Fifty Wordsigns

If you add another forty words to the initial ten common words you have already learned and have been practicing, you will know fifty of the most common words used in English. In fact, *50 percent of all written communication consists of these fifty words*. The forty new wordsigns and their words are listed below. Look them over quickly. Do you notice any patterns, any common symbols?

| it | l | is | s | as | s | not | n |
| was | z | will | l | have | h | with | w |

be	*b*	my	*mi*	me	*m*	were	*wr*
your	*yr*	this	*ts*	so	S	been	*b*
at	@	his	*hy*	one	1	would	*wd*
we	*ue*	which	*wh.*	if	*f*	she	*se*
on	*o*	what	*wt*	they	*ta*	or	*or*
he	*e*	from	*fr.*	had	*d*	there	*tr*
by	*bi*	are	*r*	has	*h*	her	*hr*
but	*b.*	all	*al*	very	V	an	*a*

Did you notice that the wordsigns for *have* and *has*, *is* and *as*, and *be* and *been* are exactly the same? This is not a mistake. You'll find that having several words that use the same wordsign won't cause confusion, because the context of the sentence when you read it back will clarify the meaning of the word represented.

Learn the Next Twenty Words

You'll want to learn these forty common words, but it's easier to learn about half of them at a time. First let's add the following twenty wordsigns to your present wordsign vocabulary. It's important that you learn the wordsigns for these frequently used words well enough to write them automatically. Learn them, and let your pencil or pen do the thinking for you.

it	*l*	have	*h*
was	*z*	not	*n*
is	*s*	with	*w*
will	*l*	be	*b*
as	*s*	your	*yr*

at	*@*	but	*b.*
we	*ue*	my	*mi*
on	*o*	this	*ts*
he	*e*	his	*hy*
by	*bi*	which	*wh.*

Memorize these twenty wordsigns before you proceed any further. Practice writing them many times on this page and on another sheet of paper. Notice the selective use of the period and dot.

WORDSIGN AND SYMBOL DRILL 10

Write the wordsign for each word four times. As you write, repeat each word aloud.

it   as

was   have

is   not

will   with

as   be

it   have

was   not

is   have

will   not

with	on
be	he
your	but
at	my
by	which
on	this
he	his
by	my
at	it
we	was

is   with

will   be

as   your

have   we

not   on

WORDSIGN AND SYMBOL DRILL 11

This time, push yourself for speed a bit. Write the wordsign for each word as often as space permits, repeating each word aloud as you write.

it   be

is   at

as   on

not   by

my	your
his	we
it	he
is	but
as	this
not	which
be	was
was	will
will	have
have	with
with	your

WORDSIGN AND SYMBOL DRILL 12

Now, using wordsigns, practice writing these words in combinations. How fast can you complete the list? Write each combination twice.

1. it was as

2. which will be

3. but by my

4. this is his

5. will be your

6. he is on

7. not at but

8. we have not

9. be with my

10. which is it

11. it is not

12. was this your

13. was he at

14. is this his

15. is he my

16. will not your

17. as will be

18. as by this

19. have we at

20. have not which

21. not with my

22. with his was

Write the following phrases twice each in wordsigns. If you find any words for which you have not been given a wordsign, simply write them out in longhand, using your rapid writing alphabet.

23. up with people

24. the way to

25. which one was

26. this is my

27. for less than

28. but we can't

29. we're greater than

30. that was all

31. he could have

32. less than ours

33. a bit not

34. therefore he will

35. we have to

36. we're greater than

37. that was all

38. to my house

39. check on his

40. with not a

41. have you heard

42. but for this

43. I will not

44. with my check

45. his was up

46. I was down

47. will we be

48. his and my

WORDSIGN AND SYMBOL DRILL 13

Now for a quick review to see if you can remember the wordsigns you have been practicing up to this point. This drill combines everything you have learned so far. Write the wordsign for each word twice. Watch your penmanship but write quickly.

up	I
the	under
which	it
you	of
this	is
for	the
but	as
greater than	to
that	not
he	be
less than	at
a	and
therefore	your
we	up
to	greater than
was	a
down	was

you   we

is   the

and   will

his   less than

which   and

therefore

WORDSIGN AND SYMBOL DRILL 14

Is it becoming easier to write the wordsigns without first having to stop and think? The more you practice, the more natural and rapid your writing will be. Write each of the following pairs of words in their wordsign equivalents. Time yourself and when you finish, write them again. See how much faster you can write them the second time.

1. over with

2. by my

3. he and

4. to your

5. check over

6. I therefore

7. be a

8. he that

9. you will

10. we have

11. which was

12. down my

13. greater than

Wordsign and Symbol Drill 15

Under each sentence, rewrite the complete sentence in wordsigns. Concentrate on the accurate formation of wordsigns and rapid writing letters. Remember: use rapid writing longhand if you haven't yet learned the wordsign for a word.

1. He ran up and down the staircase.

2. We went over the hill to my friend's house.

3. In the yard was the cat on a bench.

4. Therefore, he that is not here will not be dismissed.

5. My aunt is in that store with my uncle.

6. He thinks that he is greater than everyone else.

7. Which of the dogs will win?

8. He sat by my sister at the game.

9. Was he your friend before the accident?

10. You will have to check in your baggage over there.

11. A while ago, I saw his face in the window.

    Now, write a sentence of your own below that combines as many rapid writing wordsigns as you can.

WORDSIGN AND SYMBOL DRILL 16

The following phrases contain many words for which you have already learned symbols. Write these phrases in wordsigns and rapid writing longhand.

1. you will be   5. and it was

2. the dog was   6. which of you

3. that will be   7. you saw this

4. I have not   8. at that time

9. by the moment

10. on this paper

11. for as much

12. my sister will

13. the mouse was

14. it was nice

15. and I will

16. is this it

17. a little on

18. have you written

19. in that house

20. be not that

21. your power to

22. at which of

23. that he was

24. we will be

25. on this day

26. he went to

27. by his will

28. but which is

29. by this was

30. for we have

31. and which I

32. to my friend

33. of this cake

34. as we wait

35. will you be

36. to have you

37. not that way

38. I am with

39. I saw it

40. and to the

41. you must be

42. this is that

43. which was his

44. you have finished

Try rapid-writing these phrases. Is it getting easier to write faster? Your pen will soon be a blazing streak across the pages as you transcribe everything in wordsigns and symbols.

WORDSIGN AND SYMBOL DRILL 17

To check how well you can transcribe rapid writing, write out each of these wordsign phrases in longhand.

1. *ulb*
2. \ *dog* z
3. *te l b*
4. *e h w*
5. / *l* z
6. *wh f w*
7. *u saw te*
8. @ *te lime*
9. *b \ moment*
10. *o te paper*
11. 4 *s much*
12. *mi sister l*
13. \ *mouse* z
14. *l* z *nice*
15. / *u l*
16. *s te L*
17. *f te kake*
18. *s ue wael*

19. *l u b*
20. 2 *h u*
21. *w te way*
22. *e am w*
23. · *litle o*
24. *h u wrilen*
25. *n te house*
26. *b w te*
27. *yu power* 2
28. @ *wh. f*
29. *te e* z
30. *ue l b*
31. *o te day*
32. *e went* 2
33. *b hz l*
34. *b· wh. s*
35. *m te* z
36. 4 *ue h*

37.	/ wh. ı		41.	u must b
38.	2 mi fruend		42.	ts s u
39.	ı saw L		43.	wh. z bz
40.	/ 2 \		44.	u L finished

Check your answers with the preceding Wordsign and Symbol Drill 16 on pp. 67–69.

WORDSIGN AND SYMBOL DRILL 18

Write the symbols as fast as you can for the following words.

the	that
and	you
of	for
to	up
I	down
a	check
in	over

under	with
therefore	be
greater than	your
less than	at
and	we
was	on
is	he
will	by
as	but
have	my
not	this

his	will
which	was
it	is
which	as
this	not
but	be
he	at
we	on
your	by
with	my
have	

Now try to create your own sentence from this list of words, then rewrite it using wordsigns, using the space below. How many of the wordsigns can you use in one sentence?

The Final Twenty Words

By now, you have learned wordsigns for thirty of the fifty most frequently written words in English. Listed below with their wordsigns are the remaining twenty words. Learn them. Remember that these fifty words make up 50 percent of all written English. When you have learned to substitute wordsigns for all fifty words, you will have at least doubled your writing speed.

what	*wl*		has	*h*
from	*fr.*		very	*V*
are	*r*		were	*wr*
all	*al*		been	*b*
me	*m*		would	*wd*
so	*S*		she	*Se*
one	*1*		or	*or*
if	*f*		there	*tr*
they	*ta*		her	*hr*
had	*d*		an	*a*

Notice the selective use of the period and dot. These aren't typos. Did you notice that the wordsign for *she* begins with a capital *S*? With your pen or pencil, trace each wordsign and write it twice next to the original wordsign. Carefully practice these wordsigns below before turning the page.

WORDSIGN AND SYMBOL DRILL 19

Write the wordsign for each word at least four times. Remember, as you write, repeat each word aloud.

what	me
from	so
are	one
all	if
me	they
what	had
from	so
are	me
all	so

one

if

they

had

has

very

were

been

would

has

very

were

been

would

her

an

has

very

were

been

would	an
she	from
or	all
there	so
her	if

Wordsign and Symbol Drill 20

Using the correctly formed wordsigns, write each of these phrases at least twice. Remember that you learn by doing.

from what	if they
are all	they had
what me	has very
so one	they were

had been   one would

would she   if very

or there   they are

so her   had she

from an   has all

what if   were been

they are   would she

all had   her so

me or   what from

so there   all me

so one

one if

they had

she been

has what

all very

were all

been from

would so

she what

or if

there they

her from

so an

what has

from very

are were

all been

me would

so she

one or   if they

if there   from an

they her   has very

had an   were so

she would   would she

been if   she or

what very   or there

all from   her an

so what   would if

WORDSIGN AND SYMBOL DRILL 21

As quickly as possible, write the word represented by each wordsign. Circle the wordsign for any word you are unsure of, or don't write anything for that wordsign.

a	a	fr.
hr	hr	wl
tr	tr	a
or	or	hr
se	se	tr
wd	wd	or
b	b	se
wr	wr	wd
v	v	b
h	h	wr
d	d	v
ta	ta	h
f	f	d
1	1	ta
s	s	f
m	m	1
a	a	s
r	r	m
fr.		a
wl		

r

fr.

wl

a

hr

tr

or

Se

wd

b

wr

✓

h

d

ta

f

1

s

WORDSIGN AND SYMBOL DRILL 22

Write out in longhand the following wordsign phrases.

1.   wl fr.

2.   r a

3.   m S

4.   f 1

5.   ta d

6.   h ✓

7.   wr b

8.   wd Se

9.   Or tr

10.   hr a

11.   wl h

12.   fr. ✓

13.   r wr

14.   a b

15.   m wd

16.   S Se

17.   1 or

18.   f tr

19.	*ta hr*	32.	*ta fr.*
20.	*d a*	33.	*f r*
21.	*h d*	34.	*1 a*
22.	*ta v*	35.	*S m*
23.	*f we*	36.	*a h*
24.	*1 t*	37.	*hr v*
25.	*S wd*	38.	*tr wr*
26.	*m Se*	39.	*Or t*
27.	*a or*	40.	*Se wd*
28.	*r tr*	41.	*wl fr*
29.	*fr. hr*	42.	*r a*
30.	*wl a*	43.	*m S*
31.	*d wl*	44.	*f 1*

Check your answers on the next page.

Answers to Wordsign and Symbol Drill 22

1. what from
2. are all
3. me so
4. if one
5. they had
6. have (or has) very
7. were been (or has)
8. would she
9. or there
10. her an
11. what have (or has)
12. from very
13. are were
14. all been (or be)
15. me would
16. so she
17. one or
18. if there
19. they her
20. had an
21. have (or has) had
22. they very

23. if were
24. one been (or be)
25. so would
26. me she
27. all or
28. are there
29. from her
30. what an
31. had what
32. they from
33. if are
34. one all
35. so me
36. an have (or has)
37. her very
38. there were
39. or been (or be)
40. she would
41. what from
42. are all
43. me so
44. if one

Now try this: starting with number 44, work backward and write the rapid writing wordsign for each of these phrases. You should be beginning to feel comfortable writing these wordsigns.

WORDSIGN AND SYMBOL DRILL 23

This exercise combines all the wordsigns you have learned so far. Write the symbol for each word at least twice.

in   had   they   have

will   you   greater than   with

if	from	very	down
check	a	which	of
and	less than	the	I
your	are	up	was
one	he	been	it
me	that	she	not
so	but	would	be
you	has	there	and
we	were	an	greater than
therefore	for	or	what
all	this	her	all

are	one	at	his
less than	they	to	there
in	me	a	which
over	if	were	as
I	had	you	therefore
on	that	been	an
by	under	is	we
my	has	would	her
a	up	and	the
so	very	she	will

WORDSIGN AND SYMBOL DRILL 24

Try this exercise to see how well you've learned all fifty wordsigns for the fifty most frequently used words. All fifty words are included below. Note the ones that give you trouble and work extra on learning them. I have also included a few of those familiar "symbol" words, such as over *and* under.

the	you	greater than
and	for	less than
of	up	of
to	down	from
I	check	are
a	over	all
in	under	me
that	therefore	so

one	there	or
if	her	her
they	an	an
had	all	there
has	from	she
very	what	been
were	if	very
been	had	from
would	were	me
she	has	one
or	would	they

WORDSIGN AND SYMBOL DRILL 25

Continue practicing your wordsigns by transcribing the following phrases into wordsigns.

1. what you need

2. are you in

3. from all of

4. in an instant

5. it for me

6. one you had

7. so I would

8. if that were

9. had I been

10. they were there

11. in a very

12. she has been

13. and you were

14. I have been

15. she would not

16. an opera would

17. or all of

18. there is a

19. her task for

20. on all her

21. if they had

22. is he there

23. all would be

24. we are so

25. that is an

26. you would have

27. all in a

28. all that she

29. but not me

30. by my will

31. they made your

32. at that they

33. what will she

34. I had the

35. and would he

36. don't be with

37. and if the

38. so let me

39. have they been

43. we all but

40. or very soon

44. which is on

41. if her father

45. so all or

42. but there have

46. they had this

Answers to Wordsign and Symbol Drill 25

1. *wl u need*

13. *l u ur*

2. *r u n*

14. *u h b*

3. *fr. a f*

15. *se wd n*

4. *n a instant*

16. *a opera wd*

5. *L 4 m*

17. *or a f*

6. *1 u d*

18. *tr s.*

7. *S u wd*

19. *h task 4*

8. *f tu ur*

20. *o a h*

9. *d u b*

21. *f ta d*

10. *ta wa tr*

22. *s e tr*

11. *n . v*

23. *a wd b*

12. *Se h b*

24. *ue r S*

25. tu s a
26. u wd h
27. a/ n.
28. a/ tu se
29. b. w m
30. bi m l
31. ta made yr
32. @ tu ta
33. wl l se
34. e d /
35. / wd e
36. don't b w
37. / f \
38. S let m
39. h ta b
40. or v soon
41. f hr father
42. b. tr h
43. ue a/ b.
44. wh. s o
45. S a/ or
46. ta d Ta

Wordsign and Symbol Drill 26

Many of the following phrases are commonly used in writing—and some would never appear, but they all provide practice for you. Write each phrase in wordsigns between the columns or in the space below each phrase.

one and all

which were all

would have been

you and I

so be it   his or her

you are it   if there are

this and that   from what are

check with me   they all were

that will be   on my by

they had an   but over that

what are all   will had in

if they had   they have you

they were very   with check if

which was it   your and one

me so you

we all therefore

all from a

are what he

that less than

has but that

were for this

the very which

she been up

would there an

or her down

I was of

was it from

be not at

what all are

less than over

WORDSIGN AND SYMBOL DRILL 27

Beneath each sentence rewrite the sentence using wordsigns.

1. If her father comes, I will have to go.

2. I think that they have had this long enough.

3. So you must bring all or none.

4. That cabin is on the way to my house.

5. We all but forgot to bring the money.

6. But there have been many times like these.

7. If he doesn't come very soon, we will have to leave.

8. Have they been getting you down?

9. And do you think he would do it?

10. What will she think of me if I tell her?

11. You would have to say that to me.

12. We are so lucky to have friends like you.

13. If you will go, then I will come.

14. She has been up to the top but he has not.

15. The stereo is the best of my many toys.

WORDSIGN AND SYMBOL DRILL 28

This exercise is the last of the wordsign and symbol drills. Write the wordsign under each word as fast and as accurately as you can.

it	not	on	his
was	with	he	which
is	be	by	what
will	your	but	from
as	at	my	are
have	we	this	all

me	would	I	under
so	she	a	therefore
one	or	in	greater
if	there	that	less than
they	her	you	it
had	an	for	was
has	the	up	is
very	and	down	will
were	of	check	as
been	to	over	have

not	my	one	this
with	than	if	there
be	his	they	her
your	which	had	an
at	what	has	the
we	from	very	and
on	are	were	of
he	all	been	to
by	me	would	I
but	so	she	a

in	for	therefore	less than

that	up	greater than	or it

you	over

A Final Retention and Review Exercise

On the following pages you will find 100 practice sentences.

Using the first fifty sentences, practice transcribing the words into wordsigns. If you have not learned a wordsign for a particular word, write it longhand using your rapid writing letters. When you have finished, check your accuracy by referring to the following pages where the sentences have been written in wordsigns. These wordsign sentences—the first set of sentences that you have seen written completely in rapid writing—are written following the rules of rapid writing that you have learned to this point, and that you are going to learn in the next chapter of this book. Notice how easy some of them are to interpret even though you have not yet learned how the sentences were turned into rapid writing.

The second set of fifty sentences are written in wordsigns. Since you may not know many of the words in each sentence, see how rapidly you can spot and transcribe into longhand those that you have learned. Can you make out any of the words or sentences that you have not yet learned? Check your accuracy by looking at the answer pages. By the way, not all of these sentences make sense, but they use many of the "famous fifty."

SET 1: TRANSCRIBE INTO WORDSIGNS

1. A balloon has the ability to light on air.

2. There is an alternative to every situation.

3. The soldier was accused of avoiding work.

4. The advertisers gave their answer weeks ago.

5. That avenue was an awkward road to take.

6. Anyone could see that the Americans were winning.

7. She worked until school started in August.

8. April is appreciated after a hard winter.

9. My husband is not available at this time.

10. My aunt arrived at the Atlantic Ocean last night.

11. The bedroom was one of the most beautiful ones I had seen.

12. He was very talented in basketball.

13. You will see a queen in that room.

14. The baggage arrived soon after we did.

15. His Bible is black, but mine is blue.

16. We had egg with tomato for breakfast.

17. My brother is buying a new car.

18. The bottle was broken in a little box.

19. The breeze brings aid to the community.

20. Mother was busily making a buttonhole when I came into the house.

21. The story of the bombing was mailed in a telegram.

22. Our cabin on the mountain was closed at sunset.

23. The children were quite chilly after the long walk.

24. My church provided attention last year.

25. Our class was the first to get home.

26. Such circumstances were difficult to believe.

27. They all had cigarettes before leaving.

28. This chicken was chosen over the rest.

29. The chandelier was bobbing chaotically.

30. The change could not be taken calmly.

31. The cat bolted under the chesterfield.

32. Our close circle of friends went to the office today.

33. The cake was eaten by the great crowd.

34. He conducted the business with great confidence.

35. My creativity was crushed by his shout.

36. How could he see the end of the corridor?

37. He coughed crazily for hours.

38. The cornerstone of the community was Columbus.

39. Her knowledge was conclusive of collapse.

40. The dancer was known for her performance.

41. The darkness looked quite dangerous.

42. It was the dawning of a new day.

43. The democracy made no demands on its citizens.

44. He was determined to win despite the diagnosis.

45. The design did justice to the room.

46. He had a definite problem with digestion.

47. The disappointment was too great to beat.

48. We were given the right directions.

49. The doctor was discovered to be a failure.

50. Try to compose a new piece of newspaper.

Set 1: Wordsign Answers

1. . blln h \ abl⁻ 2 ll o ar

2. Tr s a allrnv 2 err slan

3. \ sldr z akuz f avdg wrk

4. \ ad rz gv tr ansr wka ago

5. Tr arnu z a awkwrd rd 2 lk

6. Ny 1 kd c Tl \ Amrknz wr wng

7. Se wrk nll skl Srl⁻ n Agsl

8. Aprl s aprahal⁻ f c . rd unbr

9. ni hzbn a wr avll @ ts lm

10. Ti nl aru— @ \ Allnlk on l Srl

11. \ barm z 2 f \ msl blfl 1z r d cn

12. Eo z v Ulrl⁻ n bshibl

13. Ul wl c . kn n tl rm

14. \ bggag aru— sn fr ur dd

15. Hz Bbl a blk, b. mn a blu

16. ur d o wr 2mlo 4 brkfsl

17. mi brlr a big . nru kr

18. \ bll z brkn n . lll bx

19. \ brz brgz ad 2 \ kmn⁻

20. mlr z bz mkg. bllrihl w e km ~ \ hs
21. \ Sry f \ bmbg z ml n Ugrm
22. Or kbn o \ ml z klz @ snsl
23. \ cldrn wr kl cly fr \ lng wlk
24. mi cu prvd aln~ lS yr
25. Or kls z \ 1 sl 2 gl hm
26. sc srkmslnsz wr dfkll 2 blv
27. ta a d sgrlz b 4 lvg
28. ts Ckn z Czn ~ \ rsl,
29. \ cndlr z bbg kolk~
30. \ cng kd w b lkn km~
31. \ kl bl~ ~ \ Califld
32. Or kls srkl f frnz wl 2 \ ofs 2da
33. \ kk z eln bi \ grl krd
34. e kndkl~ \ bzns w grl Kfs
35. mi krlv~ z krS bi hz Sl
36. hw kd e c \ nd f \ kidr
37. e kf kz/ 4 orz
38. \ krnisln f \ kmn~ z Col
39. hr nlaz z Kklv f klps

40. \ dnsr z —n f hr pfmns
41. \ drkns lk— kl dngrs
42. L z \ dnz f . nu da
43. \ dmkrsy md — dmnds o Ts slznz
44. l z dlrmn 2 un dspl \ dgnss
45. \ dzn dd ftls 2 \ rm
46. e d . dfnl prblm w dgs n
47. \ dspnl⁴ z 2 grl 2 bl
48. Ue wr gvn \ rl drkmz
49. \ dv . z dskvr 2 b . flr.
50. lre 2 kmpz . nu ps f nzpr

SET 2: TRANSCRIBE INTO WRITTEN SENTENCES

1. . gln f gs ksls 2 mC
2. \ gm z glg 2 wld 4 m
3. Gen Us \ Sry f krln
4. Gev . s bkmg mr prgrsv w
5. \ grl z gvn . gfl 4 hr bldy
6. ta wr rkrd 2 wr oo
7. tr gl s gg 2 b dfkll 2 alv
8. tr s lll grndr asst— w r gov

9. . wf dz nt lk 2 b lkn 4 gent

10. l z . grsm sl

11. \ grs s grw-g grl ts yr

12. l snl gd 2 b . grmblr

13. Se slk . hrpn o hr hl

14. Hrld swm hp n \ pl

15. Hry kl hz hr mC 2 hsl

16. \ ndn hd'drs z brl clr

17. \ wndz wl hl evnl

18. mi hrl kd b hrd 4 mls

19. ue snl hr 2 gl hlp

20. i z hslnl abl lkg \ hwy

21. hslrns hld tl Col. dskvr Amrknz

22. tl hrn mks . hrbl snd

23. tl hrbl akst pl hm n \ hspll

24. ue a hp tl hr hsll wnl lsl lng

25. \ hrn o \ bs z v Srl

26. mi hrs lvz 2 el hl'dgz

27. \ hl hshld z wl-g 4 tl hr

28. ue grw a f r vglblz n . hi'hs

29. hw dd \ hmn rs gt ~ sc . ms ?

30. \ prly hmbl bw— b4 \ dcs

31. te old mn z brn . hnt'bk

32. ue hrd rd bk 2 \ frl 2 skp \ ambs—

33. m̄ mbr us 2 h a isbx n hr hs

34. MS f hz idz wr mprvnt 2 r dsk n

35. tr idntly wl rmn . mstry 4vr

36. f O ue kd mk a mprvml o \ hs

37. a f hr vsnz wr mgnry

38. \ drs . ns n z kl mprsv

39. te kr s dnt— a nc fr . \ hd

40. Chas h a nklnt n 4 wrkg v hrd

41. fr hz ndk n, e z snl drkt 2 \ nfrm y

42. \ frk n blvn \ 2 part' hz nkrs grt

43. ue nkr 4 n 4 mn kncrng \ bby

44. e fnd a nskl nsd m nu bk

45. ts nspk n lwr— \ mrl . dgs

46. \ sgg f \ nnl anlm z kl nkra nl

47. \ nkl ue wr nsd, \ alrm snd—

48. ta wr gvn Psfk n Sknz 4 \ d g

49. *[handwritten shorthand]* nllgt ppl dnl nlrpl org knvrs nz

50. *[handwritten shorthand]* \ prfsr gv a nlr Sg nlrdk n 2 \ lkblr

Set 2: Transcription Answers

1. A gallon of gas costs too much.
2. The game was getting too wild for me.
3. Genesis tells the story of creation.
4. Germany is becoming more progressive now.
5. The girl was given a gift for her birthday.
6. They were required to wear glasses.
7. Their goal is going to be difficult to achieve.
8. There is little grandeur associated with our government.
9. A wife does not like to be taken for granted.
10. It was a gruesome sight.
11. The grass is growing great this year.
12. It isn't good to be a grumbler.
13. She stuck a hairpin on her hat.
14. Harold swam happily in the pool.
15. Harry cut his hair much too hastily.
16. The Indian headdress was brightly colored.
17. The wounds will heal eventually.
18. My heart could be heard for miles.
19. We sent her to get help.
20. I was hesitant about taking the highway.
21. Historians hold that Columbus discovered America.
22. That horn makes a horrible sound.
23. That horrible accident put him in the hospital.
24. We all hope that her hostility won't last long.
25. The horn on the bus was very shrill.
26. My horse loves to eat hot dogs.
27. The whole household was waiting for that hour.
28. We grow all of our vegetables in a hothouse.
29. How did the human race get into such a mess?
30. The party humbly bowed before the duchess.
31. That old man was born a hunchback.
32. We hurriedly rode back to the fort to escape the ambush.
33. My mother used to have an icebox in her house.

34. Most of his ideas were impertinent to our discussion.
35. Their identities will remain a mystery forever.
36. If only you could make an improvement on the house.
37. All of her visions were imaginary.
38. The doctor's incision was quite impressive.
39. That car is dented an inch from the hood.
40. Charles had an inclination for working very hard.
41. After his induction, he was sent directly to the infirmary.
42. The friction between the two parties has increased greatly.
43. We inquired for information concerning the baby.
44. I found an insect inside my new book.
45. This inspection lowered the morale a degree.
46. The singing of the national anthem was quite inspirational.
47. The instant we were inside, the alarm sounded.
48. They were given specific instructions for the dog.
49. Intelligent people don't interrupt others' conversations.
50. The professor gave an interesting introduction to the lecture.

Wordsign and Symbol Speed Test

This speed test comes in two parts.

PART I: TRANSCRIPTION

The purpose of the following test is to check your rapid writing speed and accuracy. The essay below is relatively uninspired, but each line is packed with words from your list of fifty frequently used words. Try to use symbols for the fifty words for which you have learned wordsigns; one word will be subtracted from your score for each wordsign you do not use. If you haven't learned a wordsign for a word, simply write the word out, using the streamlined rapid writing alphabet.

Beginning with the following paragraph, write below each line just as you did with the Gettysburg Address speed test. Write as quickly as you can, but remember that you must be able to read back everything you have written. Complete the entire test. Time yourself.

Beginning time _____

What is your objective in learning to write faster: Is it   **7**

to keep up with teachers who are entranced with their own   **5**

lectures, or with conference speakers who tell old jokes and   **5**

recite motivational sayings? Perhaps you would like to take   **3**

fuller notes at meetings that you attend. Whatever your purpose   **4**

may be in working through this book, you will be amazed at the   **8**

rate of increase of your writing speed by the time you have   **7**

finished this book. Every exercise you do helps your speed. As   **6**

you are taking this test you will be using your new skills. If   **8**

you have diligently done your exercises to this point, you will   **7**

find that it is easy for you to remember the wordsigns you have   **9**

learned.   **0**

It is not possible to increase your writing speed if you   **7**

merely look at this book. You must work to increase your skills.   **5**

One of the best ways to increase your speed is by practicing all   **8**

the wordsigns you have learned by using them whenever you can.   **5**

Don't hesitate to use rapid writing techniques right now in your   **4**

meetings, the office, in classes. As your friends and co-workers   **4**

no longer see your head bent for long periods of time over a pen   **5**

and paper, they will begin to wonder how you write so fast. You   **8**

will begin to find that you have more time to listen than before.   **7**

Instead of writing, you will be able to think about what you have   **8**

written. While others are still scribbling away, you will be   **4**

able to relax.   **1**

If you are wondering why your pen is not zooming across the   6

page faster than it is, you must remember that there are lessons   7

in the next few pages that, by themselves, will double the speed   6

at which you are now writing. Just be sure that you are writing   7

legibly and that you are using all the wordsigns that you have   9

learned.   0

Rapid writing will become one of your best friends.   4

Lectures will no longer be tedious, for you will be able to sit   7

back and listen to what the speaker is saying without struggling   5

to take down all that is said. In being able to think about a   6

lecture while you are there, instead of only taking down notes,   4

the material and the message of a speaker become relevant and   6

meaningful.   0

If you have a busy schedule, like me, but do not want to be   **9**

limited in your activities, rapid writing will help you save   **4**

time. You will be able to reread and study your notes for   **7**

reports and exams much faster.   **1**

All you must do now is not become discouraged or neglect   **7**

your rapid writing exercise on days which are busy for you. It   **5**

only takes a few minutes to do them, but the rewards that you   **6**

will have from them are worth more hours than you will be able to   **8**

count. So just keep exercising and practicing, and you will find   **5**

yourself becoming an expert rapid writer with your new skills.   **3**

Ending time _____

To find your total time, subtract your beginning time from your ending time. Now divide 483 (which is the total number of words) by your total time rounded to the nearest quarter minute. For example, if your total time is 14 minutes, your score is 34.5 words per minute (wpm).

Next, determine your errors in the following way. Count the number of wordsigns you used in each line. The number you should have used is printed to the right of each line. Subtract one for each wordsign you missed. Add your errors from each line to get your total number of errors.

wpm: _____

Errors: _____

How well did you do? The chart below gives you a general idea of how you are progressing.

Number of Errors	Rating
5 or fewer	Good job
6–10	Average
11 or more	You need more practice

PART II: DICTATION

For this part, you will need someone to assist you. Ask your "volunteer" to read this same essay to you while you attempt to copy it down on a piece of paper as quickly as you are able. When you are finished with this "dictation" test, calculate your writing speed the same way you did with Part I. Also, try reading your transcription back to the person assisting you while he or she follows along in the essay to see if you captured the majority of what was being "dictated" to you. Are you faster when you take dictation or when you are copying from a book? Don't forget to check yourself the same way you did in Part I to determine if you missed any wordsigns.

A Quick Summary and a Look Ahead

Up to this point you have learned to use two very important tools to speed up your writing: the rapid writing alphabet, and the wordsigns and symbols for the fifty most frequently used words. The next chapter of this book emphasizes the importance of "sound" writing and omitting unnecessary letters. By these two methods you will create new wordsigns to add to those you already know. Study this next section carefully.

STEP 4

Omit Letters in Words to Increase Your Writing Speed

Omit needless words.

Vigorous writing is concise. A sentence should contain no unnecessary words, a paragraph no unnecessary sentences, for the same reason that a drawing should have no unnecessary lines and a machine no unnecessary parts.

—WILLIAM STRUNK, JR., *The Elements of Style*, 1918

John Moschitta recited 545 words in 55.8 seconds, or 586 words per minute, on May 24, 1988 in Los Angeles, California.

You have now streamlined your rapid writing alphabet, and you have learned the wordsigns or symbols for the fifty most frequently used words as well as several other words for which you already knew a familiar symbol. Just that alone may enable you to double your writing speed for much of what you write. But what about all those other words that you have to write, words that aren't among the fast fifty you've already learned?

You need to know how to trim the size of *every* word you write, and you need to be able to do this in such a consistent manner that you don't even have to think about it; you just do it.

Fortunately, you've come to the right book, because in the next several pages you're going to learn how to reduce words to their most essential components by omitting all unnecessary letters. This new instruction won't take you long to read, nor will it take you very long to understand. It's

119

really very simple. But, you should know that after you read about it, you must practice applying your new learning in order to *acquire* your new skills and make it a natural part of your rapid writing, so don't skip the drills in this chapter.

Omit All Unnecessary Letters From Words

A very important general rule in rapid writing is to omit all unnecessary letters when you write. You should include only the letters necessary for reading and understanding what you write. Leave off any letters that aren't absolutely essential for conveying the meaning of a word. For example, what could be more unnecessary that those extra letters in the names of the months (*Jan* ,

Aug. , *Nov.* , *Dec.*), the states (*Io.* , *Tenn.* , *Ark*), our past presidents (*Wash.* ,

Lin. , *Ken.* , *Ny.*), the points of a compass (*N* , *S* , *E* , *W*), or cities (*N.Y.* ,

Det. , *Phil.* , *Den* , *L.A.*). If you stay aware that many words are easily identi-

fiable even when there are letters missing, you'll find ways to shorten the words you're writing. Just remember two very important rules:

Rule One: Omit All Vowels

Although vowels give words their distinctive sounds, they are not as essential to word recognition as consonants. Look at the following sentence:

y-- c-n r--d w-rds w-th v-w-ls l-ft --t.

Now try the same line with the consonants pulled:

-ou -a- -ea- -o--- -i-- -o-e-- -e-- ou-.

As you can see, even though it's difficult to make any sense of words when the consonants are removed, the vowels can be left out entirely and you can still "read" and make sense of what's left. For example, what could be more unnecessary than the vowel in this word? *mlk* The word is *milk*, of course. Thus, the word *despite* will be written *dspt* and the word *history* will appear *hstry*.

But what about words like *dine* and *lake*? *Dine* or *den* could be represented by *dn*, and *lk* could be *lake* or *like* or *look*. At first glance, it appears we could have some confusion here, but not really. This leads us to Rule 2.

Rule Two: Let Context Determine Meaning

In nearly every case, the context of the word will determine the word meaning if a wordsign looks as if it could mean more than one thing. For instance, in the case of the two words above, if the sentence in which the two words are found says, "We are going to *dn* when we get back from the *lk*," there is little chance that you will read it as, "We are going to *den* (or *dune* or *done*) when we get back from the *like*." It is almost impossible to think of a sentence in which *dune* or *den* or *dine* or *done* can be used interchangeably.

The sand dn felt soft underfoot

Using *den* makes a creative but improbable statement. And *done*, of course, is grammatically incorrect.

But what about a situation like this:

The fall damaged his bk

In this case, where *back* or *bike* or even *book* would fit, and where the context won't give you much of a clue, go ahead and include the proper vowel. *Don't be handcuffed by a rule if following it brings confusion.* Spell out any words that are troublesome. Don't waste time trying to figure out how to remove vowels or any other letters when the result would be a troublesome or confusing wordsign—just write all the letters and move on. Ninety-nine percent of the time there will be no confusion.

Always Write the Word As It Sounds

We've mentioned it briefly earlier in this book, but this point is so important it needs to be emphasized: write each word as it *sounds*, not the way it is correctly spelled.

Certain words lend themselves very well to being written the way they sound. For example, *day* da , *two, too,* and *to* 2 , *enough* $enuf$, *love* lv , and *colonel* $krnl$.

Other words do not lend themselves quite so easily to "sound" writing. They may take a bit of effort. For example, *laboratories* $lbrbz$, *explain* $Xpln$, and *arithmetic* $math$.

Breaking Your "Good Speller" Habit

Keep in mind that whether the words you're writing lend themselves easily to being written the way they sound or whether they take a bit of effort, what's important is that you break the pattern of spelling correctly when you rapid-write. That desire to spell everything correctly has been ingrained by dozens of teachers and years of careful attention to your spelling.

But you don't need to worry that somehow this "sound" writing is going to turn you into a bad speller when you write normally. It just doesn't happen. You're fully capable of abbreviating words, leaving out vowels, and spelling things the way they sound when you're rapid-writing, and then spelling things properly at other times.

Focus on Clarity, Not Consistency

At about this point in your practice you may sometimes write different wordsigns for the same words. Don't worry.

You're still learning, practicing, and exploring different ways to reduce your writing to a bare minimum. Weeks from now, after you've been using your newly acquired skill for some time, and after rapid writing has become a habit, you'll find that your rapid writing has fallen into some patterns and your wordsigns have become consistent. At this stage in your learning, focus on clarity and penmanship. Be certain that you don't abbreviate and shorten too much and make your wordsigns unreadable in your rush to learn to write faster.

Follow These Rapid Writing Guidelines

Periodically, you need to stop and take time to evaluate your progress and remind yourself of the basic rapid writing rules.

1. *Make haste slowly.* Concentrate on correctness, and speed will follow. It's useless if you write so rapidly and carelessly that you cannot transcribe the wordsigns you've written.

2. *Write neatly.* Here are four handwriting flaws to avoid.

   A. *Illegible numbers.* Watch out for your numbers. Sometimes our numbers—specifically 5, 0, and 2—are unreadable.

   B. *Illegible letters.* Forty-five percent of all handwriting errors involve four letters: a, e, r, t.

   C. *Writing e like i.* Fifteen percent of all handwriting errors involve the confusion of these two letters. In rapid writing, keep the loop open in the e, closed in the i. It's your only clue.

   D. *Letter formation.* There are three commonly recurring errors in rapid writing letter formation:

      1) Failure to close letters like a and d.

      2) Closing loops in letters like b and f.

      3) Putting loops in nonloop letters like t and p.

3. *Don't stop to think.* If you forget a wordsign, don't stop to think about it. Keep writing, and if necessary write the word out in full.

4. *Practice.* In developing a skill like rapid writing, much practice is essential. Do the drills for at least thirty minutes a day. Practice until the wordsigns come to mind as quickly as their longhand counterparts.

Letter Omission Drills

The following drills are very important to your success in learning rapid writing. You will want to do them all.

One last thing: don't worry about transcribing each word in these drills "correctly." Different people will transcribe words differently. Some will remove more letters than others but still be able to read their transcriptions correctly. You should be developing a *personal* system of rapid writing that works for you.

OMISSION DRILL 1

Using the rules for omitting letters that you just learned, transcribe each word below several times into a wordsign. In this exercise and the ones that follow, remember that the rapid writing alphabet does not contain the letter c. *Substitute* k *if it is a hard sound as in* color *and* s *if it is a soft sound as in* century. *Remember: write the words the way they* sound.

read	feel
road	knife
day	leave
fine	fumble
better	veal
aim	high
accuse	rye

sat	oak
few	attorney
knew	inside
upon	reside
upper	school
does	river
sew	house
dine	team
usual	voice
said	please
climb	maybe
drink	can
beat	week

about	accommodate
against	queer
purpose	oatmeal
pneumonia	square
horse	even
yacht	cat

See, that was both easy and fun. Now, slowly and carefully go back over your wordsigns looking at them for "extra" letters. Could you have omitted any additional letters and still read what you had written? If you want to check to see how I would write the wordsigns for these words, look up the words in Appendix B, the glossary.

Note: *When you check your wordsigns against those in the glossary, you may see some glossary wordsigns with strange beginnings or endings. At this point don't worry about those. In the next chapter you're going to learn some simple wordsigns that can be used for common beginnings (prefixes) and endings (suffixes) of words.*

OMISSION DRILL 2

Relax for a few minutes before you begin this drill. Your goal with this drill again is to see how quickly you can reduce each word to its wordsign equivalent. After you've finished, if you wish to check your wordsigns against the suggested wordsign equivalents, look up the words in the glossary in Appendix B.

breeze	more	twenty
absence	eat	must
dancer	major	movement
grumbler	avenue	money
advice	library	reader
tutor	balloon	conclude
animal	grass	root
hostile	kept	fight
four	investigate	try
officer	pool	away

valley	write	mistake
mountain	row	sleigh
slope	blue	act
climb	crowd	bed

Now go back over each wordsign and look at it to see if you could have abbreviated it even more while still being able to read and interpret it easily. Do this for all of the drills in this book.

Omission Drill 3

Transcribe each phrase below, using the initial fifty frequent word wordsigns and the omission techniques you have learned. If you have not been given a wordsign for a new word, create your own wordsign. Write the word as you think it sounds, and don't be concerned if your wordsigns for new words aren't exactly like those in the glossary; you'll learn some more shortcuts later. Be sure to leave out all unnecessary vowels and consonants. Also remember: you must be able to read back whatever you transcribe after it gets "cold."

1. telling the man

2. upsetting her vase

3. reducing some tension

4. hastily recalling memories

5. momentarily the car was stalled

6. without delay he ran ahead

7. intelligent research was made

8. confirming the rendezvous

9. filled with contemptible thoughts

10. carelessly running through the fields

11. those unfortunate circumstances

12. composing an elaborate design

13. fearfully withdrawing from the race

14. bringing about absolute attention

15. society's pressures engulfing him

16. risking one's position

17. while singing in the rain

18. after a short meeting

19. thoughts that are filled

20. always a writer's prerogative

Now, cover the left-hand side of this drill with a piece of paper and read back the phrases you've written. If you can't read some of them, make up different wordsigns for those phrases, perhaps simply by adding a letter. Try to get the meaning of difficult words from the context of the phrase.

OMISSION DRILL 4

Transcribe each phrase into wordsigns, leaving out any unnecessary letters, especially vowels.

1. box office history

2. which it took

3. with good reason

4. the masterful acting

5. into this film

6. portraying the transformation

7. an old man

8. hot-headed son

9. his father's successor

10. considered nature itself

11. equally beautiful paintings

12. approaching a view

13. participating in activities

14. protect the group

15. influence on society

16. goodness, peace, and perfection

17. providing political protection

18. discussion of business

19. power vacuum within

20. lacked understanding of business

21. marked for respectability

22. despite his own inclination

23. carrying out instructions

24. maintaining their identities

Omission Drill 5

Transcribe the following sentences into wordsigns. Remember to do what you've learned so far to speed your rapid writing, and don't end your wordsign sentences with a period. In rapid writing, a larger than normal space between sentences indicates where one sentence ends and the next one begins. Just leaving out periods will shave seconds off your rapid writing and note taking.

1. Without any warning, he bolted through the door and interrupted us.

2. No one can slander life, who has not experienced death.

3. We played in the fields, running and laughing as if we were children.

4. There is always something to be learned in every situation.

5. Education and learning help one to look within oneself.

6. The only measure of success is improvement.

7. Growth means change and, therefore, cannot be explained.

8. In everyone's life there are shadows that disappear with the dawning of a

    new day.

9. No person can escape the reflection of his or her own soul.

10. Grandeur is impressive, but simple things touch the heart.

11. Time is a gift that can be appreciated or taken for granted.

12. All men may be created equal, but their attitudes toward equality make

    them differ.

13. People are free only if they believe in themselves.

14. The lightheartedness of a child comes from the absence of worry over self-

    image.

15. Words are spoken to communicate or to fill awkward silences.

16. Silence can become an inspiration to finding one's own soul.

17. The written word gives time for contemplation.

18. Maturity comes through problems that have been resolved.

19. Nothing would ever be accomplished without persistence.

20. The ideas for great works are admired but useless, if they are not accom-

    panied by hard work.

21. Within each person there is a greatness that is waiting to be discovered.

22. Understanding is learned only through disappointments and failures.

23. All good things are twice as beautiful when they are shared.

24. Depending on others will only stifle one's originality.

25. Rain washes away memories from the sidewalk of life.

26. Learning comes easier when experience is the teacher.

27. You can lead a horse to water, but you cannot make it drink.

28. Today is the first day of the rest of your life, so make it count.

29. Man can tame the wildest animals, but he is unable to tame his tongue.

30. Tomorrow may be too late to do what we should have done yesterday.

31. Every night, as I watch the sun setting, I am reminded of her.

32. If we cannot live for today, how can we ever hope to face tomorrow?

33. There have been continuous attacks to the north, which have resulted in

    increased bombing.

34. The Europeans are more advanced culturally than the Americans.

35. There are many false notions which preoccupy the human understanding.

36. It has been said that we search for knowledge in lesser worlds and not in

    the greater or common world.

Now go back and read the sentences aloud, looking only at the wordsign sentences. If you can't read the sentences back smoothly, write them one more time on another sheet of paper. Do you see any places where you could have abbreviated but didn't?

OMISSION DRILL 6

Write the following sentence in longhand *as often as you can in two minutes. Then count the number of words you have written and record that number at the bottom of the page.*

In mastering a skill like rapid writing, a person facilitates learning for himself or herself by saving a lot of time usually spent on the mechanics of writing.

Number of words _____

Now write the same sentence as often as you can in wordsigns *for two minutes and record your word count.*

In mastering a skill like rapid writing, a person facilitates learning for himself or herself by saving a lot of time usually spent on the mechanics of writing.

Number of words _____

Did you find that you could write the sentence many more times using rapid writing?

OMISSION DRILL 7

Try the procedure in Omission Drill 6 again, this time using different sentences. Write the following two sentences as often as you can in longhand for one minute each. Then do the same thing using wordsigns. Which way enables you to write the sentences more often?

Now is the time for all good men to come to the aid of their country.

Learning to rapid-write will enable you to spend more of your time listening than writing.

OMISSION DRILL 8

To become more fluent in reading back your wordsigns, transcribe into word-signs the following section from the poem "Endymion," by John Keats. Use as few letters as possible. In doing this and the following drills, be sure to substitute k or s for c. With this drill, don't write on this page. Write your wordsigns on a separate piece of paper.

> A thing of beauty is a joy forever:
> Its loveliness increases; it will never
> Pass into nothingness; but still will keep
> A bower quiet for us, and a sleep
> Full of sweet dreams, and health, and quiet breathing.
> Therefore, on every morrow, are we wreathing
> A flowery band to bind us to the earth,
> Spite of despondence, of the inhuman dearth of noble
> Natures, of the gloomy days,
> Of all the unhealthy and o'er-darkened ways
> Made for our searching: yes, in spite of all,
> Some shape of beauty moves away the pall
> From our dark spirits. Such the sun, the moon,
> Trees old, and young, sprouting a shady boon
> For simple sheep; and such are daffodils
> With the green world they live in; and clear rills
> That for themselves a cooling covert make
> 'Gainst the hot season; the mid forest brake
> Rich with a sprinkling of fair musk-rose blooms:
> And such too is the grandeur of the dooms
> We have imagined for the mighty dead;
> All the lovely tales that we have heard or read:
> An endless fountain of immortal drink,
> Pouring unto us from the heaven's brink.

Now read aloud what you've written. Can you easily read the poem by reading your transcription? Would it have been possible to abbreviate or omit more letters in some words and still maintain clarity and understanding? Remember, the more letters you leave out, the faster you'll write.

OMISSION DRILL 9

The following sentences have been written in wordsigns. Perhaps some of these wordsigns do not look exactly like those you have been creating or like those in the glossary, but don't let that concern you at this point. Read the sentences aloud as fast as possible.

1. Evryur e lrnd, e fasd a ml selns

2. \ wrdz ↑o tl prntld pg bkm prt f hm

3. Lrning bkmg ledus unls tr s . prps

4. D lrmnshn s \ grlst fklr n bkmng sucsful

5. Bd bgnngs kn bkm chllngz 2rd mprvmnl

6. Evry prsn strls oul dremng, b. only sm lrn drmz n2 rlly

7. Wzdm kn b lrnsl only thr Xprns

8. Frndshp s w smthng tl kn b dmndd; l s 2 b gvn

9. \ msl nlrslng ppl r those w mnny nlrsls

10. Wn ea prsn tr s krlvrly tl nds 2 b dskvrd

Omission Drill 10

Try to create wordsigns for as many of the words in these "speaker-like" sentences as you can. Push yourself for speed, but don't sacrifice clarity and your ability to read back your wordsigns.

1. Everywhere he turned, he faced an empty silence.

2. The words upon that printed page became part of him.

3. Learning becomes tedious unless there is a purpose.

4. Determination is the greatest factor in becoming successful.

5. Bad beginnings can become challenges toward improvement.

6. Every person starts out dreaming, but only some turn dreams into reality.

7. Wisdom can be learned only through experience.

8. Friendship is not something that can be demanded; it is to be given.

9. The most interesting people are those with many interests.

10. Within each person there is creativity that needs to be discovered.

(You can check the sentences in Drill 10 against the wordsigns in Drill 9.)

Omission Drill 11

Write out in wordsigns the following "literary-like" sentences.

1. All night long, men moved through the darkness outside their tents like

   tongueless wraiths with cigarettes.

2. The unfrosted lightbulb overhead was swinging crazily on its loose wire,

   and the jumbled black shadows kept swirling and bobbing chaotically, so

   that the entire tent seemed to be reeling.

3. The girls had shelter and food as long as they wanted to stay.

4. Each day he faced was another dangerous mission against mortality.

5. A doctor with a large forehead and horn-rimmed glasses soon arrived at a

   diagnosis.

6. His talented roommate was obviously a person to be studied and emulated.

7. The father stood very rigid and quaint in a double-breasted suit with

   padded shoulders that were much too tight on him.

8. There was a gruesome and excruciating silence that threatened to endure

forever.

9. He was a person who never tanned, and he kept out of the sun as much as

possible to avoid burning.

10. Standing just over nine feet in height and weighing nearly seventeen

hundred pounds, the mother Kodiak knew that she could take on and

defeat any one of the males face-to-face.

OMISSION DRILL 12

Try to read and write out each of these wordsign sentences. Don't rush. These sentences are designed to be a bit trickier and more challenging than the ones you've practiced up to this point. Notice how the more you work with these wordsigns the easier it gets to "interpret" them. The longhand versions of these sentences follow.

1. *[handwritten shorthand]*

2. *[handwritten shorthand]*

3. $15 - 8 = 7$

4. *[handwritten shorthand]*

5. *[handwritten shorthand]*

6. *[handwritten shorthand]*

7. Lz . mstk 2 Sk tl oz knd

8. e pz— mmnbr 2 rmmbr smlg mprtnl

9. u Sdnl alwz b S Ksrn— w mnl vlg

10. hz mbr bksm mr / mr mprtnl 2 hm

11. tl ml . tr kd b mvl

12. \ mvml f \ ms ske— mi sslr

13. e mw— \ grs 2 ml / l de

14. hw fsl ksn u mllp tz nmbrz 2glr

15. mi nrlw z Czn a \ olrz

16. r n n hz fnd l nssry 2 g 2 wr

17. e d nwr d . nkls 64

18. e nd . nu dl ts yr

19. de z Sns tl de ddnl sm rl

20. tl nl z S blfl tl el nwr 4gl l

21. \ byz km nz / \ rm / sl ↓

22. \ brdz hw gn nrl agn nw tl org hz km

23. tr z nlg de kd d abl \ nzbld

24. grndmlr d . fny n n abl Nov

25. u mol lk . nmbr / wl yr krn

26. \ sl ok z dl ↓ lS mnl

27. e Sv \ olíml ∼ hz ml / grml
28. \ Urz objh∽z wr aluz hl obvs
29. okz∼n \ on ld Sa ol a da
30. tl id d nvr okr 2 m
31. tr z a mbrs∽g or n \ ofs
32. Od. s 1 f \ mS blfl mols f \ yr
33. \ ofor z v srkslk n hz ksl∼g
34. Se kdnl oml ny mprl t fkls f \ nvl
35. e h b 2 ○ 1 opra
36. ue skz∼ orngz 4 brkfsl ta mrn∽g
37. \ orgnza∼n orgnl d ○ 12 mmbrz
38. ― or Sdnl d se orgnl t
39. e z 1 oz ∽ \ rkr∼ wl
40. l∼ S kld olsd tl \ pdlz h frzn
41. e lld m tl e hl∼ m ⊙ agn
42. e lks lk . dlkl∼ n tl O'kl
43. \ bby z 2 daz Od
44. ue Oslml∼ hz abl t 2 kp w \ sla∼n
45. \ fac. on s 100 mlz fr . mi ln
46. \ pnl∽g z h∽ng n . fm∽ mz∼m

47. *Se 1 \ sl Cmprісp σ \ pill brz*

48. *e z gvn a awrd 4 prlopalg n \ evnl*

49. *· plrn 4 Ts nsd t h b sl n \ pS*

50. *\ pvt d b brk n svrl plsg*

Longhand Version

1. That mile never seemed quite so long before.
2. If you want to be a milkman, you probably won't make a million.
3. Fifteen minus eight equals seven.
4. Minute by minute he came closer to splashdown.
5. There were miscellaneous articles on the women's page.
6. Sometimes great misery can be seen in a mission.
7. It was a mistake to shake that man's hand.
8. He paused momentarily to remember something important.
9. You shouldn't always be so concerned with monetary values.
10. His mother became more and more important to him.
11. That mountain over there could be movable.
12. The movement of the mouse scared my sister.
13. He mowed the grass too much and it died.
14. How fast can you multiply these numbers together?
15. My narrative was chosen over all the others.
16. Our nation has found it necessary to go to war.
17. I had never had a necklace before.
18. I need a new coat this year.
19. She was so nice that she didn't seem real.
20. That night was so beautiful that I'll never forget it.
21. The boys came noisily into the room and sat down.
22. The birds have gone north again now that spring has come.
23. There was nothing she could do about the nosebleed.
24. Grandmother had a funny notion about November.
25. You must take a number and wait your turn.
26. The stately oak was cut down last month.
27. He shoved the oatmeal into his mouth and grunted.

28. The teacher's objectives were always quite obvious.
29. Occasionally the ocean tide stayed out all day.
30. That idea had never occurred to me.
31. There was an embarrassing odor in the office.
32. October is one of the most beautiful months of the year.
33. The officer was very sarcastic in his questioning.
34. She couldn't omit any important facts of the novel.
35. I have been to only one opera.
36. We squeezed oranges for breakfast this morning.
37. The organization originally had only twelve members.
38. No other student had such originality.
39. He was one ounce under the required weight.
40. It is so cold outside that the puddles have frozen.
41. He told me that he hated me over and over again.
42. He looks like a detective in that overcoat.
43. The baby was two days overdue.
44. We overestimated his ability to cope with the situation.
45. The Pacific Ocean is one hundred miles from my town.
46. The painting was hung in a famous museum.
47. She won the state championship on the parallel bars.
48. He was given an award for participating in the event.
49. A pattern for this incident has been set in the past.
50. The pavement had been cracked in several places.

Summary

In this chapter you learned that you should omit all unnecessary letters, especially vowels, from words when you're rapid-writing. In addition, you were instructed to ignore "correct" spelling when you rapid-write and to write words the way they sound. These important instructions need to be recalled frequently as you attempt to establish reliable patterns for doubling and even tripling your writing rate.

STEP 5

Squeeze Valuable Minutes Out of Plurals, Possessives, Abbreviations, Prefixes, Suffixes, and Capital Letters

> *Quick speed is good.*
>
> —ROBERT GREENE

In the first four chapters of this book, you learned how to use the three most important tools for speeding up your writing: a streamlined alphabet, word-signs (for the fifty most frequently used words in the English language), and shorter words (with omitted letters).

In this chapter, you're going to learn several other techniques to add to your repertoire. You'll learn how to speed up the writing of plurals, possessives, and prefixes and suffixes; how to use capital letters selectively; and how to save time through the use of abbreviations.

Indicating Plurals and Possessives

Plurals

English language rules of grammar and syntax indicate that the plural form of a word is usually formed by adding an *s* or *es* to the singular form. The plural form of boy is boys; the plural form of church is churches.

In rapid writing, however, a plural is indicated by adding a *z* to the singular form. The wordsign plural for *cat* becomes *klz* ; the wordsign plural for

churches becomes *CrCz* . Simple, right? Just add the letter *z* and you have made any and every word plural.

Possessives

How then do we indicate the possessive form of a word? For example, what if we wanted to write "The boy's car was red" in rapid writing wordsigns? In longhand, we'd add an apostrophe to indicate possession, whether it's one boy's car or two boys' car.

However, in rapid writing you don't indicate possession with any mark at all. It isn't necessary when you're relying on the context of the sentence to indicate meaning. Ninety-nine percent of the time, you'll be able to tell from the context whether a word is possessive. For example, read the following word-sign sentence:

\ *drz wndo z krk*

(The door's window was cracked.)

See how easy it was to determine possession from the context?

Try writing the wordsign for each of the plurals listed below. You won't be able to tell whether the wordsigns show possession, because there is no context for each word.

absences	churches	times
advertisers	directorships	tomatoes
afterthoughts	historians	unions

treasurers	lessons	problems
umbrellas	libraries	queens
uncles	machines	railroads
vegetables	maids	outsiders
questions	maybes	populations
stations	millions	potatoes
telegrams	sisters	replies
instances	societies	restaurants
invitations	squares	revolutions
kings	stamps	sandwiches
kitchens	states	senators
laboratories	prejudices	rivers
lakes	presidents	overcoats

offices	democracies	struggles
oranges	chocolates	worlds
medicines	circumstances	works
miles	centuries	nations
mothers	years	governments
circles	fathers	honors
extras	portions	measures
editions	places	devotions

Using Familiar Abbreviations and Creating Your Own

All rapid writing words are, of course, abbreviated. As we discussed earlier, there are also many common standard abbreviations in English that may be incorporated into your rapid writing techniques. But wait—how do you tell an abbreviation from a wordsign when you read it?

Use a period. Since you don't use a period with the wordsigns and wordsign sentences you've been writing, a period will clearly indicate an abbreviation. When a period follows a wordsign, that means "Treat this word differently. Don't try to figure out which vowels have been left out. This is an abbreviation."

Use the old standbys. Such abbreviations as bldg., A.M., and P.M. are old standbys. Use them and other familiar abbreviations whenever possible, but don't confine yourself to these.

Invent your own. Make up abbreviations, especially for technical or professional and vocation-related words that you find yourself writing frequently.

Limit the length. Try to limit the length of any abbreviations you invent to just one syllable, usually the first syllable, but if the syllable isn't suggestive enough as in the case of the words *anonymous* or *university* (the letters *an* or *u* would not be much help standing by themselves), then add an extra letter or syllable to make the abbreviations clear. Then end the abbreviation with a period.

Keep the apostrophe in mind. If you can utilize an apostrophe to indicate a special abbreviation, do it. For example, a common abbreviation for the word *Christ* is X. A good way to indicate the word *Christian* is to use that abbreviation and the apostrophe X'n to form *Christian*.

Listed below are some relatively common abbreviations. Some of them could be shortened even more if you wanted to learn a shorter version. Notice how the presence of the period keeps you from trying to read them as wordsigns.

adjective	*adj.*	graduate	*grad.*
adverb	*adv.*	important	*imp.*
American	*Amer.*	inch	*in.*
Christ	X	junior	*jr.*
corporation	*Corp.*	man	♂
dollar	$	masculine	*masc.*
especially	*esp.*	medicine	*med.*
estimated	*est.*	miscellaneous	*misc.*
feminine	*fem.*	mister	*mr.*
following	*ff.*	modern	*mod.*
Genesis	*Gen.*	occasionally	*occas.*

originally	*orig.*	professor	*prof.*
ounce	*oz.*	railroad	*rr.*
page	*p.*	regarding	*re.*
pages	*pp.*	road	*rd.*
population	*pop.*	therefore	∴
pound	*lb.*	woman	♀

What other common abbreviations can you think of?

ABBREVIATIONS DRILL 1

Using the suggested abbreviations from above, write the abbreviations for the following words. Can you write the abbreviations from memory?

woman	especially	man
adjective	pages	important
road	feminine	junior
American	ounce	adverb
railroad	occasionally	Christ
corporation	Genesis	dollar
professor	medicine	estimated

following	pound	modern
graduate	population	masculine
inch	page	mister
therefore	originally	miscellaneous
regarding		

ABBREVIATIONS DRILL 2

Make up your own abbreviations for the following words. Your abbreviations do not necessarily have to begin with the first two or three letters. Symbols like $, &, and # are good to use also.

continually	introduction	class
government	divide	finally
senior	business	first
citizen	meeting	middle
bibliography	answer	group

before	teacher	fortunate
only	appointment	each
once	equal	English
end	continued	out
parallel	within	hour
twice	power	without
spelling	omit	sometimes
insert	into	vegetable

ABBREVIATIONS DRILL 3

Using the abbreviations already suggested, abbreviate the following words. Write the wordsign abbreviation for each word at least three times as you repeat it aloud. Push yourself for speed this time.

corporation	page
medicine	pound
originally	railroad
graduate	dollar
estimated	Christ
junior	pages
adjective	modern
feminine	following
inch	American
regarding	mister

especially   population

Genesis   miscellaneous

occasionally   man

professor   appointment

ABBREVIATIONS DRILL 4

Make up your own two-, three-, or four-letter wordsign abbreviations for the following words. Suggested abbreviations appear in the glossary, Appendix B, if you really get stumped.

know   window   tomorrow

forgotten   hospital   circle

flower   bottle   company

manner   bandage   potatoes

breakfast   gallon   black

percent	avenue	corridor
blue	square	quality
minus	week	question
moment	perfect	collapse
forward	italics	figure
egg	arithmetic	dangerous
rubber	plus	mathematics
empty	edition	number
quotation	multiply	glasses
tomato	education	pattern

ABBREVIATIONS DRILL 5

Write out the following phrases by combining wordsigns you already know with new wordsign abbreviations. Be sure that you're able to read them back. Note: Write your wordsign transcription to the right of each phrase, not underneath it.

1. therefore he continually

2. before the introduction

3. in the middle of Genesis

4. only an inch

5. sometimes he was forgotten

6. she continued telling the answer

7. five pages of adjectives

8. being without a bibliography

9. especially teaching medicine

10. the class was without a teacher

11. the appointment on the hour

12. multiply the middle number

13. first came the introduction

14. a quotation on being American

15. as a senior citizen

16. the business meeting tomorrow

17. a government without power

18. sometimes we are fortunate

19. once feminine and perfect

20. therefore he occasionally

21. a class over miscellaneous

22. a dollar a gallon

23. our modern population

24. regarding the junior professor

25. omit one page

26. the railroad company continued

27. only a pound of potatoes

28. an inch away from being equal

29. especially in Genesis

30. always a mister

31. estimated at the following

32. for a graduate education class

33. modern glasses originally

34. Christ was the medicine to heal

35. in the middle of the page

36. insert at the end of the bibliography

37. business and government are parallel

38. the moment of introduction

39. the first meeting without his group

40. the mathematics of percent

41. before you answer the question

42. once in a while omit

43. twice she used eggs and tomatoes

44. don't forget the end

45. only sometimes do those pages

46. a street, avenue, or circle

47. plus a dollar a pound

48. no citizen without equal education

49. a perfect blue flower

50. a one-percent figure

Now check your wordsign abbreviations against the previous pages of exercises on abbreviations to see if you used the same wordsign abbreviations. You'll have trouble reading back your writing if it's inconsistent. Now cover the left-hand column of this exercise and read aloud the phrases you have written.

ABBREVIATIONS DRILL 6

In this drill, try to be consistent in the abbreviations and wordsigns you use. As always, keep the following points in mind in creating new wordsigns:

1. *Omit all unnecessary letters, especially vowels.*
2. *Write the word as it sounds. Don't worry if your wordsigns for new words are not exactly like those in the glossary.*
3. *Substitute* k *or* s *for the letter* c.
4. *Transcribe as fast as you can.*

1. The government continued to crush the hopes of the population.

2. The first pages of Genesis are equally important.

3. In need of medicine, he staggered forward and collapsed by the window.

4. Twice the professor questioned the bibliography I wrote for class.

5. The answer to why the corporation collapsed is a mystery.

6. All citizens should know the important facts regarding American government.

7. The first edition contained a different introduction, bibliography, and foreword.

8. Following the class an important question-and-answer period was

conducted.

9. Population figures have been released to the groups of corporations.

10. The pages of miscellaneous figures were forgotten within a week.

11. Continued progress in medicine brings hope to every citizen.

12. The senior citizen group holds a meeting twice a week.

Now check to see if you can read each sentence back smoothly. To see if you're consistent in your abbreviations, check the abbreviations in each line for the following words.

government 1, 6	medicine 3, 11	answer 5, 8
continued 1, 11	forward 3, 7	corporation 5, 9
hopes 1, 11	collapsed 3, 5	citizen 6, 11, 12
population 1, 9	twice 4, 12	figures 9, 10
first 2, 7	question 4, 8	group 9, 12
pages 2, 10	bibliography 4, 7	week 10, 12
important 2, 6, 8	class 4, 8	

ABBREVIATIONS DRILL 7

Follow the instructions given previously for Drill 6, and transcribe the following sentences using abbreviations and wordsigns. Remember to be consistent in the abbreviations you use.

1. The teacher finally asked us to omit that number and insert another one.

2. In six days I will have the bandage removed at the hospital.

3. Fortunate is the man who knows the value of the dollar.

4. Quality education is our first but not our only goal.

5. A dollar a pound is too expensive for potatoes.

6. Multiply six percent by this number.

7. The end of the avenue was dangerous without a stop sign.

8. She finally arrived for the business appointment, even though she was an

   hour late.

9. It would be dangerous to remove the bandage first.

10. Without thinking, the man drove past the hospital and turned on Third

Avenue.

11. The quality of the potatoes was poor.

12. The hospital omitted the charge for this appointment from my bill.

13. It is dangerous to assume that the quality is high, without checking

first.

Again, check to see that you are being consistent in your abbreviations.

finally 1, 8	remove 2, 9	dangerous 7, 9, 13
omit 1, 12	hospital 2, 10, 12	without 7, 10, 13
number 1, 6	dollar 3, 5	appointment 8, 12
six 2, 6	man 3, 10	avenue 7, 10

Limit Your Use of Capital Letters

All practitioners of rapid writing agree that capital letters are large and cumbersome. They should be used sparingly, since they can decrease your rapid writing speed and consume much space. A little later in this chapter you'll learn how capital letters are used to indicate prefixes. Here, we'll focus on two additional uses of capital letters.

To indicate proper names. Proper names should be capitalized. In addition, they should be spelled out if they are unfamiliar to you. Otherwise, they can be abbreviated. Here are some samples:

Albert	*Alb.*	Harold	*Har.*	Bolivia	*Bol.*
Benjamin	*Ben.*	Richard	*Rch.*	Amsterdam	*Amd.*

To indicate days and months. The days and months should be capitalized, but since they are so familiar, they may be abbreviated as shown.

Days: *Su. M. T. W. Th. Fr. Sa.*

Plurals of days: *Sus. Ms. Ts. Ws. Ths. Frs. Sas.*

Months: *Jan. F. Mar. A. My. Ju. Jl. Au.*
Sep. O. N. D.

CAPITAL LETTERS DRILL 1

On a separate sheet of paper practice using capitals by connecting letters in the pattern shown below.

Write from *Aa* through *Zz. Aa, Ab, Ac, Ad, etc..*

CAPITAL LETTERS DRILL 2

Capitalize the following words. Abbreviate words where possible, but write out in rapid writing those which are unfamiliar to you. Write each three times.

harry	arithmetic	february
bolivia	monday	clubs
english	wednesday	gothic

monday	saturday	september
tuesday	thursday	education
april	april	organization
june	may	germany
october	sunday	january
wednesdays	october	sunday
pacific	august	friday
march	susan	cubs
december	mondays	december
washington	june	north

november	thursdays	stadium
march	sundays	tuesday
february	mister	pole
january	columbus	avenue
july	boards	saturdays
october	thursdays	sundays
august	july	july
may	november	september
saturdays	dr. james	professor
friday	mondays	queen

ABBREVIATIONS AND CAPITALS DRILL

This drill concentrates on combining the use of capitals and abbreviations, but uses all the other rapid writing techniques you have learned also. Copy the sentences below each line. Use abbreviations where you can.

William Carlos Williams (1883–1963). Educated at Horace Mann High

School, New York City, Chateau de Lancy, Switzerland, and University of

Pennsylvania Medical School. Internship followed by graduate study abroad.

After 1910 lived in Rutherford, New Jersey, where he practiced medicine until

retirement; for a time head pediatrician at Paterson General Hospital. One of

the most experimental of American free-verse poets, constantly in search of

"the line" rhythmically most natural to American speech and feeling. Dr.

Williams's career was in many ways parallel (though often counter, also) to that

of his old friend Ezra Pound, whom he met when both were students at the

University of Pennsylvania.

Learn Wordsigns for the Ten Most Common Word Beginnings

Omission of letters, abbreviations, and the selective use of capitals was mostly a matter of common sense. Now comes an element of rapid writing that is mostly a matter of memorization.

Certain letters in English tend to be used together frequently to create particular sounds in words. Certain prefixes or word beginnings are also quite common. In rapid writing what is important is the sound of the letters, not the letters themselves.

Remember, It's the Sound, Not the Letters

Listed below are the ten most common sounds and prefixes in the English language, along with their wordsigns. Carefully note that these wordsign symbols refer to *sounds*, not necessarily to *letters*. For example, the word *chemical* begins with the letters *ch*, but the sound of these two letters is different from the sound of *ch* in *chapter* or *church*. *Chemical* would be rapid-written *kmkl* because the *ch* has the sound of *k*. The word *chandelier* also begins with *ch*, but the word would be rapid-written *Sndlr* because the initial *sound* is *sh*.

Sound	Symbol	Example	
1. sh	* s*	shell	*Sl*
2. ch	C	church	*CrC*
3. st	S	stolen	*Soln*
4. over	*O* or ⌒	overdue	*Odu*
5. under	*U* or ⌣	underwear	*Uwr*

Sound	Symbol	Example	
6. sub	↙	sublet	*Sll*
7. th	t	them	*tm*
8. con	K	control	*Klrl*
9. sp	ⱷ	spring	*Prng*
10. with	W	withdrawn	*Wdrw*

Note: The wordsign symbol for *sp* may be described as a small *s* with a capital *P* superimposed on it: ↙   ⱷ   ⱷ

English words incorporate these letter combinations and word beginnings so often that you should know them thoroughly if you want to increase your rapid writing skills. Practice writing the wordsigns for each sound at the same time as you pronounce it.

BEGINNINGS DRILL 1

Write each word in wordsign form as often as space permits. Use the "beginnings" symbols shown to the left.

1. sh =   sheet   show

            shake   shave

2. ch =   chicken   chirp

chest   chilly

3. st =   stone   street

stole   store

4. over =   overlook   overuse

overtime   overwork

5. under =   underline   underpaid

undergo   underwater

6. sub =   substitute   substance

subsidy   subject

7. th =   this   theater

	thanks	theft

8. con =   confer   conceit

conform   conclude

9. sp =   spoon   spent

split   spirit

10. with =   withdraw   within

without   withhold

BEGINNINGS DRILL 2

Write the following words in wordsigns several times each, using the new "beginnings" symbols.

override   overlap

overpower   overhand

sherbet	subjective
shingle	splash
shepherd	spoil
shaver	spider
stocking	spaced
stitch	chance
sterilize	chicken
standard	choose
suburban	consider
substance	conflict

undercurrent

thunder

thread

thirteen

thorough

theory

underneath

undermine

underdog

underfoot

withholding

withal

withdrawn

wither

withheld

spell

special

concede

control

through

thin   underweight

submarine   chesterfield

sublime

BEGINNINGS DRILL 3

Write the following words two times each. If necessary, you may check back on the previous pages to see if you're using the right symbol for the beginning of each word.

shallow   sublease

shout   thinking

challenge   consider

station   spartan

overestimate   withstand

underwear   change

overpower	undersea
overtime	thwart
sharing	continue
wither	charge
understudy	starve
theology	overhaul
contingent	underhanded
chatter	submit
within	theme
thick	consistent

spring	stoic
withal	spinning
shame	undervalue
still	shiver
sublimate	steel
chosen	sparse
subjective	submission
overseer	contend

Learn Wordsigns for the Ten Most Common Word Endings

You have seen how much "beginnings" symbols can shorten words and increase your rapid writing speed. Now do the same with word endings.

As was true with "beginnings," certain letters are often used together at the ends of words to create particular sounds. We don't care which *letters* are being used, but we care which *sounds* the words end with. And the *sound*, not necessarily the letters of the word, is what the symbol represents. For example, the last four letters in *ocean* have the sound *shun*, and the last four letters in *onion* have the sound *yun*, and we use one wordsign to represent that sound. The word *sensory*, even though it ends in *ory*, has the sound *ery*.

The ten most common word ending sounds, along with their symbols, are listed below. The rule to remember for indicating the symbol for a common ending is: extend the end. The stretched-out-looking last letter indicates a commonly used "ending" sound.

Sound	Symbol		Example
1. ing	~*g*	*b~g*	= buying
2. shun, zhun, yun	~*n*	*f~n*	= fashion
3. ent, ment, dent	~*t*	*eqp~t*	= equipment
4. live, sive	~*v*	*cp~v*	= captive
5. ery, iry, ary	~*y*	*lrs~y*	= treasury
6. ter, ture, ther, tor, der, dor	~*r*	*mo~r*	= mother
7. able, ible	~*l*	*la~l*	= table
8. ity	~*i*	*myr~i*	= majority
9. ed	—	*eqp—*	= equipped
10. ily, ley, ly	*)*	*ll/*	= lately

Memorize these sounds and their symbols before you turn the page. Note that some words such as "mother" and "motor" are written the same way. The meaning of the wordsign *mor~* is determined by context.

ENDINGS DRILL 1

Write each word in wordsigns as often as space permits. Remember to use "beginnings" symbols and abbreviations also, as well as the new "endings" symbols.

1. ing =   going   nothing

                        calling   giving

2. shun, zhun, yun = information   ocean

                        location   incision

3. ent, ment, dent = accident   resident

                        experiment   placement

4. tive, sive =   attentive   alternative

                        responsive   cursive

5. ery, iry, ary =   imaginary   necessary

                        every   summary

6. ter, ture, ther,   brother   picture

    tor, der, dor =   border   nature

7. able, ible =   capable   visible

    legible   passable

8. ity =   facility   formality

    utility   locality

9. ed =   inquired   loaned

    wired   moved

10. ly, ily, ley =   quickly   busily

    noisily   socially

Be sure that your endings for the ed *sound do not look like your endings for* ry, ily, ley, *and* ly.

ENDINGS DRILL 2

Write each word in wordsigns at least three times.

receiving	relation
permanent	fidelity
every	adornment
valley	primary
showed	thunder
ability	impertinent
daughter	artillery
ladder	calmly
present	classed

lovable	master
torture	happily
odor	electricity
president	movable
sewing	mother
formality	attentive
indent	decision
necessary	monetary
digestion	walked
inventive	massive

overture	picture
adoption	passive
objective	moment
actor	misery
practiced	mowed
community	creative
Bible	sister

Those Tricky Compound Words

Compound words are not hard to rapid-write, but they are hard to read back unless you know that they are compound words. For example, this wordsign *whfl*, could be difficult to read. However, if you write the wordsign this way *whfl*, it's easier to see *waterfall*. To indicate that a wordsign represents a compound word, all you have to do is place an apostrophe after the first word in the compound word. Be certain to place the apostrophe only *after* writing the wordsign, not while writing, otherwise you slow yourself down unnecessarily. For this guideline to work efficiently, one of the words in the compound word, most often the first word, should be easily abbreviated.

Indicate repetitions by circling the word or symbol.

evergreen	*e'grn*
cornerstone	*krnr'stn*
headdress	*hd'drs*
meantime	*mn'tm*
everlasting	*e'lstg*
broadcast	*b'cst*
buttonhole	*b'hol*
more and more	⊕
year after year	(yr)

COMPOUND WORDS DRILL 1

Transcribe the following compound words into wordsigns. Make sure that you distinguish between repetitions and compounds. Remember to use all the rapid writing techniques you've learned.

over and over   lodestone

without   setback

chimney sweeper   hay fever

dunghill

coat of arms

close-up

cold-blooded

day after day

scrapbook

pepperbox

less and less

Dutchman

Pullman

ultramarine

dustpan

hundredfold

hothouse

huntsman

tenderhearted

somewhat

forever

household

servicewoman

living room	towboat
fatherland	hunchbacked
combat team	minute by minute
clothespress	topcoat
nosebleed	purebred
northland	stoplight
scoutmaster	ultranationalism
stoneware	stockpile
toss-up	featherweight

COMPOUND WORDS DRILL 2

Transcribe the following compound words into wordsigns as you did on the previous drill.

lighthouse	shoestring
rowboat	hot dog
everything	dust mop
bedspread	icebox
somewhere	hairpin
toothpaste	scarecrow
basketball	postcard
sunset	necklace
rainbow	crowbar
thunderbolt	popcorn

driveway   football

airplane   baseball

pillowcase   freeway

dishwasher   raincoat

stopwatch   overpass

mailman   bunk bed

throughout   milkman

restroom   checkbook

anyone   highway

overcoat   bedroom

earring   keyboard

field house   turtleneck

sailboat   upstairs

stairway   fingernail

You may check your wordsigns for these two drills against the Glossary, Appendix B.

Tips for Increasing Speed

Up to this point you have been concentrating on accuracy, legibility, and consistency in your rapid writing. These three points are still vitally important, but you should now be experienced enough to profit from some suggestions on speed improvement.

1. Write with as few strokes as possible

Look for ways to simplify and improve your rapid writing. Practitioners of rapid writing frequently develop their own variations and improvements on what they learn in this book. Keep looking for ways to speed up your rapid writing over the next several months.

2. Write small

It may seem like a little thing, but you'll cover less space and gain time if you write small.

3. Don't dot your *i*'s and *j*'s, and don't cross your *t*'s

Don't forget to work at breaking these writing habits when you're rapid-writing. Those dots and lines are unnecessary and take longer to write.

4. Don't erase or keep crossing out

If you make a mistake, strike through it once and keep writing. A lot of unnecessary time can be lost with erasing and obliterating your mistakes.

5. Practice, practice, practice

Those are the three most important words of advice for increasing your rapid writing speed.

BEGINNINGS AND ENDINGS TEST

Using the beginnings and endings symbols you have just learned, as well as all the other rapid writing techniques, write the following exercise in rapid writing wordsigns. Time yourself.

Beginning time _____

Overlooking the suburb of Shument, we saw a massive construction project

taking place. It seemed impossible that such a project as we were witnessing

should take place in our small community. Daily, the construction workers put

in overtime in order to complete the building project. Without any hesitation

we asked the workers what the ultimate aim of this noisy confusion was

intended to be. Finally it was discovered by one of our members that a hospital was going to rise from the huge iron foundation that had been set up. Naturally

this helped calm our hostility toward the noise and filth that was invading our

once quiet suburban lifestyle.

Over our coffee cups we discussed the negative aspects that we would have

to undergo during the building of the hospital. But when the final completion

was made and the infirmary was opened, the novelty of our complaints wore

off and it became boring to chatter idly over what we had suffered. With that,

our town became as quiet and boring as it had always been.

Ending time ———————

Divide 176 words by the total minutes (to the nearest fifteen seconds) spent transcribing to determine your words-per-minute rate.

RETENTION AND REVIEW EXERCISE

Here are 100 more sentences for your practice and review. These are a little more complex than the 100 sentences you did in the last chapter, but you now have more rapid writing skills to deal with these complexities.

As you proceed through these exercises, notice how much easier it is to think of the wordsigns now than it was when you started. The more practice in rapid writing that you get, the more efficient your writing skills become.

Transcribe these first fifty sentences into wordsigns.

1. It was quite an invitation to the inventive student.

2. James quit his new job in January.

3. June and July are my favorite months of the year.

4. His essay was filled with jumbled thoughts.

5. Just as I became a junior, the catalog was changed.

6. The keyboard should be kept free of dust.

7. It is certainly hard to find a king that is also kind.

8. You know where the kitchen is, don't you?

9. A knife was used to chop off his head.

10. He lacked the knowledge to work in a laboratory.

11. You hold the ladder while I close the window.

12. There is a large lake twenty miles east of town.

13. Lately he has always been last to finish eating.

14. This could hardly be termed a laughing matter.

15. The leader will help the children learn to read.

16. Don't leave without going to the store first.

17. Can you tell the difference between left and right?

18. His handwriting was just barely legible.

19. I have never been in a library in my life.

20. The light shone less and less through the shades.

21. Her lightheartedness was like that of a bird.

22. There are many difficult lessons to learn in life.

23. That lighthouse has been very useful.

24. I listened until I fell asleep from exhaustion.

25. There seemed to be little to live for after his death.

26. We have a small comfortable living room.

27. I loaned her my coat for the evening.

28. This locality is not my favorite.

29. This knot is so loose that I can untie it.

30. The child became lost in the empty lot.

31. The lovable puppy was lucky to find a home.

32. This machine can replace ten workers.

33. The mailman made two trips today.

34. Maintaining a household is a full-time job.

35. The majority will have to decide this matter.

36. How much does that man make a year?

37. His manners were much like those of many young people.

38. The martyred saints are remembered every year at this time.

39. Mary marked all the papers with the same grade.

40. The giant looked very masculine because of his massive shoulders.

41. A woman's mate is not her master.

42. Albert shows his maturity in his decisions.

43. Mathematics was always my favorite subject.

44. In May we might see the sun more often.

45. Maybe John will come in the meantime.

46. If Harry means me, then he must be mistaken.

47. A mechanic certainly can have a dirty job.

48. A pharmacist must measure medicine very carefully.

49. Their brief meeting brought back many memories.

50. He stopped to talk in the middle of the street.

Transcriptions for the Fifty Sentences

1. L z kt a nwla n 2 \ nen ᵐ Sdᵗ
2. Ja. kt hz nu fb n Jan
3. Jn. . Jy. r mi fvrl mos. f \ yr
4. hz sa z fl— w fmbl— tls
5. fo z e bkm. jr. \ ktlg z Cng—
6. \ kbrd Sd b kpt fre f dsl
7. l s srln rd 2 fnd · kz th s als knd
8. u — wr \ ktCn s, dnl u ?
9. · nf z uz—2 Cp ff hz hd
10. e lk— \ nldg 2 wrk n · lbrlry
11. u hld \ ldr wl e kls \ wndw
12. tr s · brg lk 20 mlz E. f lwn
13. ll e h aluz b lS 2 fn del g
14. ts kd rd b brm— · lf g mlr
15. \ ldr wl hlp \ Cldrn lrn 2 rd
16. dnl lv wol g g 2 \ Sr 1 sl
17. kn u ll \ dfrns blwn lfl · rl ?
18. hz hndrl g z fo br lgbl
19. e h nvr b n · lbr n mi lf

20. \ ll Sn ls . ls bro \ Sdz

21. hr ll'hrldns z lk tl f . brd

22. br r mny dfkll lsnz 2 lrn n lf

23. tl ll'hs h b v usfl

24. i lstn— nll i fl aslp f XhS—n

25. tr sm— 2 b lll 2 lv 4 fr hz dt

26. ue h . sml kmfrll lv-grm

27. i ln— hr mi kl 4 \ evng

28. ts lkl⌐ s nr mi fvrl

29. ts w s S ls tl i kn nrl ?

30. \ Cld bkm lsl n \ mpl ll

31. \ lvl ppy z lky 2 fnd . hm

32. ts msln kn rpls 10 wrkrz

33. \ ml'mn md 2 trps 2 da

34. mnlng . hs'hld s . fl-lm jb

35. \ mjs⌐ wl h 2 dsd ts mlr

36. hw mC dz tl o⁻ mk . yr ?

37. hz mnrz wr mc lk tz f mny yng ppl

38. \ mrlr— snts r rmmbr— evry yr @ ts tm

39. ma . mrk— a \ ppry w \ sm grd

40.

41.

42.

43.

44.

45.

46.

47.

48.

49.

50.

Now transcribe the following fifty sentences into longhand.

1.

2.

3.

4.

5.

6. el f \ krz z kryg . drvr

7. hr erz r ml or hr hd s

8. e lsl a erg o \ driwa

9. l s ezr 2 lv-tn 2 wrk

10. \ nu ed f ts bk s . lsp

11. u nd . gd educ 2 gt . smn jb

12. \ elbrt blz srprz— \ gsts

13. tr r mny ell ppl n ts K—y

14. wl ls h b nvnt— sns elktrst?

15. \ evrgrn trz wr \ llS n \ frst

16. wl u lC \ Eng. lsn 2 da ?

17. l s enuf tt we h =' hr

18. \ lwbl brn bk lwrd \ robl

19. \ skp z spSly nssry ls lm

20. \ slml ls f ekp t z grl

21. O \ Eur. kd xpln \ sla n

22. \ xkrSlz Olr z a nfrlnl Xprns

23. \ Xprl z 2 Xpln r prblm

24. lr wr xlr fsllz 4 vz ez

25. m fs knnl lr ksv ezr tn hs

26. \ fkl s tl \ m n z . flr

27. ve wr Cly fr elg \ ol'ml

28. Jn h . rd fngrnl

29. Albrl z \ frwl Clngr

30. Als hl hr ha fvr

31. \ hipn nlrpl \ hlrvs nlrdk n

32. folg wl brg rlbl rslts

33. ystrdy Jn 8 . hl dg

34. Jms z ksn — abl \ kt f hs jb

35. \ wrds wr n llks

36. \ fld hs z srC b4 \ hshld

37. \ bldg z nvslgt — 4 rll y alkz

38. Se d . fn fgr

39. \ flm z fl — wl Xprsz

40. \ ☆ fnly blm —

41. Se wl 4 . flg o hr oo

42. fibl flo — bsbl ⌒ \ Ufn

43. \ fisl z ↑ sd ↓

44. Se md . gsr w hr 4'hd

45. *4ln8/ ue h . ll 4'wrd*

46. *\ km z o . 4mll*

47. *mi 4 fnln pnz arv— ystrdy*

48. *\ friwy wl clz ts wkind*

49. *r frnSp h grwn v hh/*

50. *ny frr alkz wd b fll*

Longhand Transcriptions for the Fifty Sentences

1. The class was dismissed after that problem.
2. Double the dollar before you substitute.
3. The dustpan and dust mop were in the airplane.
4. I had a dream about a Dutchman.
5. Don't call the dog until the game is over.
6. Each of the cars was carrying a driver.
7. Her ears are empty or her head is.
8. I lost an earring on the driveway.
9. It is easier to love than to work.
10. The new edition of this book is a toss-up.
11. You need a good education to get a common job.
12. The elaborate tables surprised the guests.
13. There are many eligible people in this country.
14. What else has been invented since electricity?
15. The evergreen trees were the tallest in the forest.
16. Will you teach the English lesson today?
17. It is enough that we have equality here.
18. The towboat turned back toward the rowboat.
19. The escape was especially necessary this time.
20. The estimated loss of equipment was great.

21. Only the Europeans could explain the situation.
22. The excruciating overture was an unfortunate experience.
23. The experiment was to explain our problem.
24. There were extra facilities for visitors.
25. My face cannot be conceived easier than his.
26. The fact is that the mission was a failure.
27. We were chilly after eating the oatmeal.
28. John has a hard fingernail.
29. Albert was the featherweight challenger.
30. Alice hated her hay fever.
31. The hairpin interrupted the hilarious introduction.
32. Fasting will bring reliable results.
33. Yesterday John ate a hot dog.
34. James was questioned about the quality of his job.
35. The words were in italics.
36. The field house was searched before the household.
37. The building was investigated for artillery attacks.
38. She had a fine figure.
39. The film was filled with exposures.
40. The flower finally bloomed.
41. She went for a fitting on her glasses.
42. Football followed baseball over the telephone.
43. The footstool was upside down.
44. She made a gesture with her forehead.
45. Fortunately we have a tall forward.
46. The campaign was only a formality.
47. My four fountain pens arrived yesterday.
48. The freeway will close this weekend.
49. Our friendship has grown very quickly.
50. Any further attacks would be futile.

STEP 6

Improved Listening and Note-Taking Practices Will Help Your Rapid Writing

Short words are best.

—Winston Churchill

Many of us spend between five and twenty hours a week in meetings at work listening to industry-, client-, or product-related reports and analyses. Similarly, the average college student spends between fifteen and eighteen hours a week in class listening to lectures. *If* we don't take notes but just try to listen, and *if* the person conducting the meeting or the lecture is riveting enough, and also *if* what we're hearing is interesting to us, we *may* remember 60 to 70 percent of what we hear for about an hour. Forty-eight hours later, most of us have forgotten over 90 percent of what we heard. If we're really lucky, we'll still remember that we attended the meeting or class. Unfortunately for all of us, our memories fade quickly, and our listening skills often leave much to be desired. If we're going to remember things, we need to take notes.

We Need to Become Better Listeners

This chapter of *Rapid Writing in 6 Days* will help you improve your listening skills while you learn an efficient method of note taking. Both of these skills will combine very nicely with your newly acquired rapid writing skills to permit you to get the maximum value from your time spent in meetings or classes. Let's start with your listening skills.

You *can* teach yourself to become a good listener, but you must work at it.

The following reasons make efficient listening the most difficult learning skill to master:

1. You can't control what is said, when it is said, how rapidly it is said, or how loudly (or softly) it is said.

2. You can't control the speaker's logic, argument, reasoning, or delivery, and what is being said may be uninteresting, confusing, or illogical to you.

3. Your mental processes must move through the speaker's topic at the same rate as the speaker, or you may lose chunks of information and become confused.

4. There is very little training in improving listening skills beyond teachers telling us to "pay attention" or "sit up and listen."

But there is hope. Every day, many people are able to improve their listening proficiency dramatically by focusing on the specific listening skills and procedures discussed in the next several pages.

Speaking Rate vs. Writing Rate

If you could write as quickly as people talk or lecture, you wouldn't have much trouble taking notes in meetings or class. You would just sit close enough so that you could hear, copy down *everything* that was said, and review it later to determine what was important and what wasn't. For most of us this is not possible, because we are limited in how fast we can write: about forty words per minute before we learn to rapid-write, and about eighty words per minute using rapid writing. Unfortunately, the average speaker speaks at about 125 to 150 words per minute, with rates sometimes increasing to 200 words per minute in short bursts. Obviously, even a skilled stenographer would have difficulty listening to what is being said and copying it all down. There are, however, some things you can do that will maximize your newly acquired rapid writing skills.

Recognize the Importance of Your Notes

Just listening without taking notes in meetings or class will lead to disaster. But notes will help us recall what was said. The notes you take in class or meetings are usually the best source of help for remembering and understanding the important material that was covered. The problem is that most of us are not very skilled at determining what is important in what we are hearing. Everything sounds equally important at the time, so we try to copy everything down—and it can't be done. Even with your new rapid writing skills, you will have to copy down information *selectively*. This means that you not only must attend and listen, you must take efficient notes at the same time.

Be Prepared for Taking Notes by Having the Right Tools

1. *You may want to get in the habit of keeping a note-taking notebook* if you find yourself frequently needing to take notes. Having all your notes in one organized place will prove to be very convenient. Spiral notebooks are best for several reasons. They can be purchased in different sizes so that they fit in your briefcase, purse, or file folder. Many have pockets in them where any handouts given in the meetings can be kept, so you can easily keep notes from one meeting or class separate from notes from another meeting or class.

2. *Don't use a pencil.* Notes made in pencil smear and fade on paper, often making your writing illegible; pencil points keep breaking and need to be sharpened. Instead, use a pen. Pens come in different colors, if you want to make notes stand out. The ink won't smear or fade. And pens don't require sharpening.

Follow a Note-Taking Pattern

It's important to establish an effective pattern of copying down your rapid writing notes on the page in such a way as to capture the most information in the shortest possible time, but in a *format* that doesn't need to be reorganized later.

The sample note-taking page that follows shows you an effective format for taking notes in any meeting or class. Make certain that you date each set of notes, and that you leave plenty of white space between main points. If you miss a point, leave additional blank space. You can fill in what you missed later by checking with someone else who was present. Look over this sample note-taking format carefully before you continue reading.

Comments Questions Check on		Questions/Summary: Immediately after taking notes summarize the main points, or
	I. Outline what is said if	
	A. The speaker speaks	
look up	B. Or the presentation	
?	II. Is presented in	
	Outline form	
	~~	
Due the 16th	1. If the speaker doesn't speak in outline form.	
	2. Don't attempt to outline	
!.?	3. Simply record key points	
Get more details	4. Or illustrations	1. Raise bond questions

The Center Portion

The center portion of each note-taking page is where you write your notes. Don't try to outline a talk or lecture if the speaker doesn't present material in outline format—most don't. Just copy down what appear to be the main points. Take the most complete rapid writing notes you can about each point the speaker seems to be making. Numbering different points helps to keep them separate.

The Left Column

The left-hand column on the same page should be used for your observations and reminders about the points in the lecture. You will not want to interrupt the speaker constantly with questions, but you will want to identify those parts of what is said that you have questions on and ask about them at the first opportunity. A question mark in the left column opposite a point in the talk or lecture, or a hastily written question, will remind you to raise that question or clarify a point later.

Often a speaker will indicate in some way that a piece of information is especially important, or that something mentioned in brief will need to be reconsidered at a later time. Note that fact in the left column immediately! Use this left column for any point you want to be reminded of later.

The Right Column

The narrow column on the right side of each page should be used to do one or two important things. Immediately after each meeting or class where you took notes, and while the information is still fresh in your mind, write a couple of questions or summary statements on each page that highlight the main points the speaker was making. This will give you condensed summary statements for each page of notes that you take. These summaries are great for review in the future.

How This Format Aids Note-Taking and Review

Following this note-taking format aids your note taking and review of notes in four very important ways:

1. Your note taking is organized.

2. The center column makes clear what was said, even years later.

3. The left-hand column highlights important parts of the lecture or talk and identifies potential important facts, issues, or questions.

4. The right-hand column summarizes the main points of each presentation.

Suddenly, weeks or months later, you need the information contained in your notes. If you don't have much time to prepare, first read the right-hand column *only*. This will give you an overview. Then glance down the left column, reading the information you identified at the time of taking the notes as probably important.

If you have more time to review, read the right-hand column first, without reading the center column, answering the "questions" or reviewing the summaries you have written. This will highlight what you do and don't know. Next read the center section. Take your time. Let it sink in. After this is finished, read the left-hand column. It will highlight important sections and points the speaker made.

Avoid "Scribblemania"

An important thing to remember in taking notes is that you must avoid what can be called scribblemania. Copying down important information in a rapid, messy, incoherent form does you no good at all because you won't be able to make sense out of it later. Don't try to rapid-write everything. It can't be done. Condense, sift, distill. Go after the *main* points, not *all* the points. Remember, your focus should first be on listening. The ears send the information to the brain—*then* to the hands. Listen to what is said before writing it down.

Know the Speaker

Adapt your note taking to the speaker. Some speakers will make it easy for you; others will make it difficult. If a speaker is organized in what he or she says, your notes should be organized. If the speaker is choppy, disorganized, or prone to wander, don't expect your notes to be any different. Adapt.

Remember, because you cannot write as quickly as a speaker can speak, all good notes are largely summaries of what was said. For some speakers, your notes must be as detailed as possible. In other situations, it's enough to have a broad concept of what was said. Know the speaker wherever possible.

Sit Up Front

You have heard this ever since high school, and it's still good advice. You may frequently find yourself in very large groups of listeners all trying to hear and take notes. Up front, not only is it easier to hear, it's also easier to see the speaker and to catch his or her nonverbal clues. If people are in front of you, you may be distracted. You hear better and you tend to stay more alert knowing that the majority of the group or class is behind you and aware of what you do. You'll also tend to nod off less if you are up front.

Listen for Clues

Speakers often let you know what things they feel are important—and that you will likely be expected to know. Be aware of the following statements, and others like them, that speakers make to signal important information.

- "This is important."
- "You'll need to know this."
- "You'll need to know how to do this."
- "This will be covered again later."
- "You may be tested on this."

Write these clues in your notes at the appropriate spots.

There are other important clues to watch.

1. *A change in voice.* A speaker's voice may get higher or lower, louder or softer as he or she presents important ideas.

2. *A change in rate of speaking.* Slowing down or pausing may signal an important point to come.

3. *Use of visuals.* Sometimes a speaker will use an overhead projector, chalkboard, flip chart, videotapes, or other visuals to illustrate an important point.

4. *Listing, numbering, or prioritizing.* A speaker may say "There are three major issues involved," or "The second most important trend is . . ."

5. *Body language.* Sometimes instructors give off signals about the importance of what they are saying by how they move. One person may sit casually on the corner of a desk or table when relatively unimportant things are being said, but stand and pace quickly when important points are being made.

Watch the Chalkboard or Flip Chart

If it is important enough to write on the chalkboard or flip chart, it's important enough to copy down. This information is more than likely going to be important in the future. Speakers often put on chalkboards and charts such things as important names, formulas, facts, time limits, costs, and so forth. When you record this information in your notes, highlight it, note its importance in your left-hand column, or indicate in some way that it is important, so that later when you review you will be certain to learn it thoroughly.

Challenge the Speaker

A good listener gets in the habit of challenging the speaker silently and, when necessary, aloud. This helps keep the focus on recording *only* important information. Statements like the following keep your mind and note taking efficient and are excellent ways to monitor your comprehension:

- He said *four* points, that's only *three*.
- Is that a digression?
- What is that an illustration or example of?

During Dull Moments Review and Summarize

No matter how stimulating a speaker is, there will be periods when nothing important is being presented or discussed. Use this time to quickly glance back over the notes you have taken and to summarize important points. Using these few minutes to clarify a hastily written point or to summarize several points will be of real value to you weeks later when you review.

Avoid Listening Errors

There are some listening errors that you ought to avoid. They waste time and keep you from really hearing what a speaker has to say.

1. *Don't interrupt in the middle of an explanation to say that you don't understand.* Wait until the explanation is complete; you may understand by then.

2. *Don't talk or otherwise disturb anyone else during a lecture or speech.* It is impolite, wastes your and your neighbor's time, and is guaranteed to irritate the speaker—not a good thing to do.

3. *Don't contribute your knowledge to the professor's lecture unless the professor encourages that contribution.* Ask questions, but permit the professor to complete the lecture without frequent comments from you.

4. *Don't display impatience: to speak, to be dismissed, to question.* It only distracts you and everyone else.

5. *Don't tape-record presentations instead of taking notes.* Taping presentations or class lectures is often frowned on by speakers because they know listening and learning aren't taking place when taping is, and often the tapes are not played back later, either. Record (with the speaker's permission) only when taping is your backup for active note taking.

6. *Don't believe that it's the speaker's job to "get the information to you."* It's always the listener's responsibility to get the information from the speaker.

7. *Don't let your mind wander.* Stay critically aware of all that's being said or done.

Don't Rewrite Notes

Taking notes haphazardly with the idea that you'll rewrite or type them in some sort of organized way later is a bad idea. It contributes to an ineffective pattern of note taking, and wastes valuable time recopying. Take notes properly to begin with and there is no need to recopy. Use that time for review.

LISTENING AND NOTE-TAKING DRILL 1

Many television and radio programs repeat the same one-minute commercials several times throughout the program. The next time you relax in front of your set, bring along a pen and paper. First, attempt to write out each different commercial in longhand. When a commercial repeats, write it out using wordsigns. For both versions, of course, stop writing when the commercial ends. To determine your words-per-minute score, just count the number of words you have written. Since the commercial lasts one minute, there is no further figuring. Notice how much more of the commercial you completed with rapid writing than with longhand.

Longhand, *words per minute:* _____

Rapid writing, *words per minute:* _____

LISTENING AND NOTE-TAKING DRILL 2

Repeat the "television commercial" drill that you just finished, but this time don't bother to write out the words of the commercial in longhand. Instead, divide up the rest of this page according to the suggested note-taking page format (three columns) and begin training yourself to take notes according to this organizational format. Repeat this exercise with several commercials.

LISTENING AND NOTE-TAKING DRILL 3

The following passage is from Wuthering Heights, *by Emily Brontë. Find a friend who will read the passage aloud to you. As he or she reads, use your rapid writing techniques to write down the passage on another sheet of paper. Decide before you begin whether you're going to try to record all the words, or whether you're going to record the essence of what is read. Have your friend read at a pace that is comfortable for you.*

One step brought us into the family sitting room, without any introductory lobby or passage; they call it here "the house" preeminently. It includes kitchen and parlor, generally; but I believe at Wuthering Heights the kitchen is forced to retreat altogether into another quarter: at least I distinguished a chatter of tongues, and a clatter of culinary utensils, deep within; and I observed no signs of roasting, boiling, or baking, about the huge fireplace; nor any glitter of copper saucepans and tin cullenders on the walls. One end, indeed, reflected splendidly both light and heat from ranks of immense pewter dishes, interspersed with silver jugs and tankards, towering row after row, on a vast oak dresser, to the very roof. The latter had never been underdrawn: its entire anatomy lay bare to an inquiring eye, except where a frame of wood laden with oatcakes and clusters of legs of beef, mutton, and ham concealed it. Above the chimney were sundry villainous old guns and a couple of horse pistols, and, by way of ornament, three gaudily painted canisters disposed along its ledge. The floor was of smooth, white stone; the chairs, high-backed, primitive structures, painted green: one or two heavy black ones lurking in the shade. In an arch under the dresser reposed a huge, liver-colored bitch pointer, surrounded by a swarm of squealing puppies; and other dogs haunted other recesses.

Now read aloud what you've written. Are you able to read the passage relatively smoothly and accurately as if it had been written in longhand? Continue to practice writing more from dictation or readings.

LISTENING AND NOTE-TAKING DRILL 4

The following passage is from Pride and Prejudice, *by Jane Austen. Find a friend again who will read the passage aloud to you at a comfortable pace. As the passage is read, use your rapid writing techniques to record as much of it as is necessary to retain the important information from the passage. Remember to use your suggested note-taking format.*

In consequence of an agreement between the sisters, Elizabeth wrote the next morning to her mother, to beg that the carriage might be sent for them in the course of the day. But Mrs. Bennet, who had calculated on her daughters remaining at Netherfield till the following Tuesday, which would exactly finish Jane's week, could not bring herself to receive them with pleasure before. Her answer, therefore, was not propitious, at least not to Elizabeth's wishes, for she was impatient to get home. Mrs. Bennet sent them word that they could not possibly have the carriage before Tuesday; and in her postscript it was added, that if Mr. Bingley and his sister pressed them to stay longer, she could spare them very well. Against staying longer, however, Elizabeth was positively resolved—nor did she much expect it would be asked; and fearful, on the contrary, of being considered as intruding themselves needlessly long, she urged Jane to borrow Mr. Bingley's carriage immediately, and at length it was settled that their original design of leaving Netherfield that morning should be mentioned, and the request made.

The communication excited many professions of concern; and enough was said of wishing them to stay at least till the following day to work on Jane; and till the morrow, their going was deferred. Miss Bingley was then sorry that she had proposed the delay, for her jealousy and dislike of one sister much exceeded her affection for the other.

Now read back to your reader what you've written. Have you captured the passage's essence and important details?

LISTENING AND NOTE-TAKING DRILL 5

Turn on some television news. Pretend that it's important to take notes on what is said by the TV newscasters for the entire program. See how well you can capture the factual information on all the news stories. Use your rapid writing and the recommended note-taking format. When the news program is finished, turn off the television and review your notes. Have you captured enough details that you essentially can recount the news stories accurately?

Postscript: What Next?

It seems a pity, but I do not think I can write more.

—Robert Scott

It's now up to you. You've learned several skills that will enable you to develop a personal system of alphabet shorthand. You've learned the importance of streamlining your alphabet and of writing words the way they sound rather than as they're correctly spelled. You've learned several ways to shorten words by omitting letters and in many cases substituting symbols for sounds, syllables, and entire words. You even know shortened wordsigns for the fifty most frequently used words in the English language, and you have a system for forming rapid writing plurals, possessives, abbreviations, beginning and ending sounds. Finally, you know the overall importance of listening correctly. In short, you know everything you need to know to double or triple your writing speed. The rest is up to you.

Practice and Apply

You now need to practice as much as possible, whenever possible, so that what you know about rapid writing gets translated into application. With practice and application of these skills, you will see your rapid writing proficiency grow and become second nature, easily going into action when speedy writing is called for.

Since the only way to attain rapid writing skill is to practice regularly, you should follow one or more of the suggestions listed below for a minimum of thirty minutes a day. By using rapid writing in your everyday activities, you'll reinforce and improve the skills you learn from this book.

1. If you can find a book with wide spaces between lines, transcribe the sentences into wordsigns.

2. In books of poetry, the right margin is usually very wide. Transcribe the poetry into wordsigns, line for line.

3. Under the words in newspaper and magazine ads, rewrite the advertisement copy in wordsigns.

4. Rewrite in wordsigns the dialogue in novels, short stories, and plays. If the dialogue is brief, transcribe at the ends of lines.

5. Take dictation from your television or radio. See how well you can keep up with words at conversational speed.

You've Already Learned More Than You Think

It's time now to see how much you've learned in six days. Two comparison tests follow. Take both tests and compare your speeds with the tests you took at the beginning of this book.

POST-COURSE SPEED TEST: THE GETTYSBURG ADDRESS

To find out how much your rapid writing has improved since you started this course, copy Abraham Lincoln's Gettysburg Address as quickly and as legibly as you can in rapid writing wordsigns. Write below each line. Time yourself: 267 words divided by your total writing time equals your words-per-minute rate.

Fourscore and seven years ago our fathers brought forth on this continent a

new nation, conceived in liberty, and dedicated to the proposition that all men

are created equal.

Now we are engaged in a great civil war, testing whether that nation, or any nation so conceived and so dedicated, can long endure. We are met on a great

battlefield of that war. We have come to dedicate a portion of that field as a

final resting place for those who here gave their lives that that nation might

live. It is altogether fitting and proper that we should do this.

But in a larger sense, we cannot dedicate—we cannot consecrate—we

cannot hallow—this ground. The brave men, living and dead, who struggled

here, have consecrated it far above our poor power to add or detract. The

world will little note nor long remember what we say here, but it can never

forget what they did here. It is for us, the living, rather, to be dedicated here to

the unfinished work which they who fought here have thus far so nobly

advanced. It is rather for us to be here dedicated to the great task remaining

before us—that from these honored dead we take increased devotion to that

cause for which they gave the last full measure of devotion; that we here highly resolve that these dead shall not have died in vain; that this nation, under God,

shall have a new birth of freedom; and that government of the people, by the

people, for the people, shall not perish from the earth.

POST-COURSE SPEED TEST: COMPREHENSIVE TEST

This will be your very last test in the rapid writing course. Set a clock or ask someone to time you. You have three minutes to transcribe as much as you can. Try to use all of the techniques you have learned.

You have done it. Those sleepless nights of drilling and exercising have paid

off. Having mastered the fundamentals of rapid writing, you will be able to

tackle anything. Taking notes and copying lengthy passages by hand will all

become a mere flash of the hand. In making rough drafts, your thoughts can be

put on paper as you think them. Using your rapid writing skills, you will find

your speed increasing consistently. The key words are *using* your skill and *not*

storing it away on the back-row shelves of knowledge in your brain.

Soon you will be thinking of new symbols you want to add to your vocabulary. As you become an expert in rapid writing, you will find that making up and recognizing abbreviations and wordsigns is as natural as spelling your own name.

Now you may sigh with relief that the daily exercises and drills are over. Yet, as you look back, aren't you glad you were persistent? In no time at all you will have tripled your beginning writing rate. Continuing to increase your speed is very important. Perhaps you will finally have an opportunity to reflect upon lectures and not just take notes. Instead of just busily writing down the ideas of others, you will be able to come up with ideas of your own.

If you want to continue to increase your speed after the course, try to practice your rapid writing in the following ways:

1. Make up drills in which you have to time yourself, using either sentences or short passages. By having the pressure of time behind you, you will find your speed increasing.

2. If you are interested in a specific job, hobby, or field of study such as poetry, history, or psychology, choose a piece of writing from these areas and time yourself several times each day on the same piece until you see improvement in your speed. This way, you will also be learning the words and expressions common to that field.

3. Try taking down lectures in outline form from television or radio.

4. When you read the morning newspaper, take down the outstanding facts and points in rapid writing.

If you find that these are not as helpful as you like, try to look back through your lessons and find some old drills or exercises that helped you. Then repeat

those on separate sheets of paper.

We hope that the time you have spent with the rapid writing materials has

been profitable, resulting in your improved writing speed. Although tech-

niques and the mechanics of writing are usually very restricted as to style and

form, we hope that the rapid writing rules and hints are flexible enough so that

you can adapt them to your own personal needs and writing style. As you

continue in your rapid writing career, we sincerely wish you the best of luck

and continued success.

Now count the total number of words that you have converted to wordsigns. Divide that total by 3 to obtain the number of words per minute you have written.

Words per minute _____

APPENDIX A. THE 100 MOST COMMONLY OCCURRING WORDS IN THE ENGLISH LANGUAGE

the	\	is	s	now	w	this	ts
and	/	will	l	not	n	his	hz
of	f	as	s	with	w	which	wh.
to	2	have	h	be	b	what	wl
I	ι	into	⌒	your	yr	from	fr.
a	·	look	lk	at	@	our	r
in	n	do	d	we	ue	want	wnl
that	tι	could	Cd	on	o	over	⌒
you	u	little	lll	he	e	man	♂
for	4	time	Lm	by	bι	only	○
it	∟	its	lz	but	b.	other	otr
was	z	more	mr	my	mι	make	mk

227

Word	Symbol	Word	Symbol	Word	Symbol	Word	Symbol
know	—	been	*b*	went	*wnt*	then	*tn*
get	*gt*	would	*wd*	an	*a*	about	*abt*
are	*r*	she	*se*	him	*hm*	like	*lk*
all	*a*	there	*tr*	ask	*sk*	who	*hu*
me	*m*	or	*or*	when	*wn*	any	*ny*
so	*S*	her	*hr*	am	*m.*	thing	*tg*
one	*1*	year	*yr*	out	*ot*	just	*jst*
if	*f*	than	*tn*	said	*sd*	well	*l*
they	*Ta*	don't	*dt*	their	*tr*	did	*dd*
had	*d*	can	*kn*	no	—	see	*se*
has	*h*	some	*sm*	up	↑	come	*km*
very	V	never	*vr*	them	*Tm*	two	*2*
were	*wr*	down	↓	go	*g*	back	*bk*

APPENDIX B. GLOSSARY OF WORDSIGNS AND ABBREVIATIONS USED IN THIS BOOK

A

a	.	accuse	*akuz*	advertisers	*advrlzrz*
		act	*ak*	advice	*advs*
ability	*abl*	activities	*aklvt*	after	*afr*
about	*abl*	actor	*ak r*	afterthoughts	*afr'tl*
absence	*absns*	adjective	*adj.*	against	*agnsl*
absolute	*absll*	admired	*admr—*	ago	*ago*
acceptable	*akspll*	adoption	*adp—n*	ahead	*ahd*
accident	*akst*	adore	*ar*	aid	*ad*
accommodate	*akmdl*	adornment	*adrn't*	aim	*am*
accompanied	*akmpn—*	advanced	*advns—*	airplane	*airpln*
accomplished	*akmpls—*	adverb	*adv.*	Albert	*Alb.*
		advertise	*ad.*	all	*a*

Word	Sign	Word	Sign	Word	Sign
alternative	*altrn*	asked	*ask*	bandage	*bndg*
always	*alwz*	assume	*asum*	baseball	*bs'bl*
am	*m.*	at	*@*	basketball	*bskibl*
American	*Amer.*	Atlantic Ocean	*Atl. O.*	be	*b*
Amsterdam	*Amst.*	attacks	*atks*	beat	*bt*
an	*a*	attention	*atnn*	beautiful	*btfl*
and	*/*	attentive	*atn*	became	*bkm*
animal	*anml*	attitude	*attd*	become	*bkm*
another	*anr*	attorney	*atrny*	bed	*bd*
answer	*ans*	August	*Au.*	bedroom	*bdrm*
any	*ny*	aunt	*nt*	bedspread	*bdsprd*
anyone	*ny1*	available	*avl*	been	*b*
appointment	*appt.*	avenue	*ave.*	before	*b'4*
appreciated	*aprsat*	avoid	*avd*	beginning	*bgg*
approaching	*aprcg*	away	*awa*	being	*bg*
April	*A.*	awkward	*awkwrd*	believe	*blv*
are	*r*			bench	*bnc*
arithmetic	*math.*	**B**		Benjamin	*Ben.*
arrived	*arv*	bad	*bd*	better	*btr*
artillery	*rlly*	baggage	*bggag*	Bible	*Bl*
as	*z*	balloon	*blln*	bibliography	*bibl*

bill	*bl*	busily	*bz*	challenge	*Clng*
bit	*bt*	business	*bus.*	chance	*Cns*
black	*blk*	but	*b.*	chandelier	*Sndlr*
blue	*blu*	buttonhole	*b'hol*	change	*Cng*
boards	*brds*	buying	*bg*	chaotically	*kolk*
bobbing	*bbg*	by	*bi*	chapter	*Cptr*
Bolivia	*Bol.*			charge	*Crg*
bolted	*blt*			chatter	*Chr*
bombing	*bmbg*	**C**		check	*v*
border	*brr*	cabin	*kbn*	checkbook	*v'bk*
bottle	*btl*	cake	*kk*	chemical	*kmkl*
box	*bx*	calling	*klg*	chest	*Cst*
breakfast	*brkfst*	calmly	*km*	chesterfield	*Cstrfld*
breasted	*brst*	can	*kn*	chicken	*Ckn*
breeze	*brz*	cannot	*knnt*	child	*Cld*
bring	*brg*	capable	*kpl*	children	*Cldrn*
broadcast	*b'cst*	captive	*kpv*	chilly	*Cly*
brother	*brtr*	car	*kr*	chimney	*Cmny*
bulb	*blb*	carelessly	*krls*	chirp	*Crp*
bunk bed	*bnk bd*	carrying	*kryg*	chocolate	*Cklt*
burning	*brng*	cat	*kt*	choose	*Cz*
		century	*snt*		

chosen	*Czn*	common	*kmn*	contain	*Kln*
Christ	*X*	communicate	*kmnıkl*	contemplation	*Klmpln*
church	*CrC*	community	*kmn*	contemporary	*Klmpry*
cigarettes	*sgrlz*	company	*Co.*	contemptible	*Klmptl*
circle	*O*	composing	*kmpzıg*	contend	*Kld*
circumstances	*srkmstnsz*	concede	*Ksd*	content	*Klt*
citizen	*slzn*	conceit	*Kst*	contingent	*Klngt*
class	*kls*	conceivable	*Ksvl*	continually	*Klnuly*
classed	*kls*	concisive	*Ksiv*	continue	*Klnu*
climb	*klm*	conclude	*Kkld*	continuous	*Klnus*
close-up	*klsp*	conclusive	*Kklv*	control	*Klrl*
clothespress	*klzprs*	conducted	*Kdkt*	cornerstone	*krnstn*
clubs	*klbz*	confer	*Kfr*	corporation	*Corp.*
clumsily	*klmz*	confident	*Kft*	corridor	*krdr*
coat	*kt*	confirmation	*Kfrmn*	cost	*kst*
cold	*kld*	confirming	*Kfrmg*	cough	*kf*
collapse	*klps*	conflict	*Kflk*	could	*kd*
colonel	*krnl*	conform	*Kfrm*	count	*knt*
Columbus	*Col.*	consent	*Kst*	country	*Ky*
combat	*kmbt*	consider	*Ksr*	crazily	*krz*
come	*km*	consistent	*Ksslt*	created	*krt*

Word	Sign	Word	Sign	Word	Sign
creative	krv	delay	dla	dishwasher	dšwšr
creativity	krvv	demanded	dm—	dismissed	dsms
crowbar	kr'br	democracy	dmkrsy	divide	÷
crowd	krd	depending	dpndg	do	d
crush	krš	design	dzn	doctor	dr.
cubs	kbs	despite	dspt	does	dz
culturally	kltr	determination	dtrmnn	dog	dg
cursive	krsv	detriment	dtrt	dollar	$
		devotion	dvn	done	dn

D

Word	Sign	Word	Sign	Word	Sign
		diagnosis	dgnss	don't	dt
dancer	dnsr	did	dd	door	dr
dangerous	dngrs	differ	dfr	dormant	drt
darkness	drk'ns	different	dfrt	double	dbl
daughter	dtr	digestion	dgsn	down	↓
dawning	dng	dine	dn	dream	drm
day	da	direction	drkn	dreaming	drmg
day after day	(da)	directorship	drktršp	drink	drnk
death	dt	disappear	dspr	driveway	drv'wa
December	D.	disappointment	dspntt	drove	drv
decision	dsn	discovered	dskvr	dunghill	dng'l
deductive	ddkv	discussion	dskn	dust mop	dš mp

dustpan	*dŠpn*	English	*Eng.*	expensive	*Xpnsv*
Dutchman	*DC'mn*	engulf	*nglf*	experience	*Xprns*
		enough	*enuf*	experiment	*Xprt*
E		entire	*ntr*	explain	*Xpln*
		equal	*=*	extra	*Xtr*
each	*ea.*	equality	*=t*		
earring	*erg*	equipment	*eqpt*	**F**	
ears	*erz*	equipped	*eqpt*		
easier	*ezr*	escape	*eskp*	face	*fs*
eat	*et*	especially	*esp.*	facilitates	*fslttz*
edition	*ed.*	estimated	*est.*	facility	*fslt*
education	*edvc.*	Europeans	*Erp'nz*	fact	*fkt*
egg	*O*	even	*evn*	factor	*fkr*
elaborate	*elbrt*	ever	*evr*	failure	*flr*
electricity	*elktrst*	evergreen	*e'grn*	false	*fls*
eligible	*lgl*	everlasting	*e'lstg*	fancied	*fnsd*
else	*ls*	every	*evy*	fashion	*fsn*
empty	*mt*	everyone	*evr'1*	fast	*fst*
emulated	*mult*	everything	*evr'tg*	fasting	*fstg*
enable	*nl*	everywhere	*evr'wr*	father	*fr*
end	*∿* or *⊣*	everywhere		fatherland	*fr'lnd*
endure	*ndr*	excruciating	*Xkrštg*	fearful	*frfl*

featherweight	*frwl*	food	*fd*	further	*fr*
February	*Feb.*	football	*fbl*	futility	*full*
feel	*fl*	footstool	*fstl*	future	*fur*
feminine	*fem.*	for	*4*		
few	*fu*	forehead	*4'hd*		

G

fidelity	*fdl*	forever	*4'vr*	gallon	*gal.*
field	*fld*	forgot	*4'gt*	game	*gm*
field house	*fld hs*	formality	*4'mlt*	gas	*gs*
fight	*ft*	fortunate	*4ln8*	Genesis	*Gen.*
figure	*fg*	forward	*4 wd*	Germany	*Ger.*
fill	*fl*	fostered	*fstrd*	getting	*gtg*
film	*flm*	fountain pen	*f pn*	gift	*gft*
finally	*fin.*	four	*4*	girl	*♀*
find	*fnd*	free	*fre*	given	*gvn*
finding	*fndg*	freeway	*frewa*	gives	*gv*
fine	*fn*	Friday	*Fri.*	giving	*gvg*
fingernail	*fngrnl*	friend	*frnd*	glasses	*oo*
first	*1st*	friendship	*frndSp*	go	*g*
fitting	*ftg*	from	*fr.*	goal	*gl*
flower	*✿*	function	*fnkn*	going	*gog*
following	*flg* or *ff.*	functionary	*fnkny*	good	*gd*

goodness	*gdns*	has	*h*	his	*hz*
gothic	*gtk*	hastily	*hst*	historians	*hstrnz*
government	*gvt*	hat	*ht*	history	*hstry*
graduate	*grad.*	hated	*ht*	holds	*hldz*
grandeur	*grndr*	have	*h*	honor	*onr*
granted	*grnt*	hay fever	*ha fvr*	hope	*hp*
grass	*grs*	he	*e*	horn	*ʃ*
great	*grt*	head	*hd*	horrible	*hr l*
greatness	*grtns*	headdress	*hdrs*	horse	*hrs*
group	*grp*	heal	*hl*	hospital	*hsptl*
growth	*grwt*	heard	*hrd*	hostile	*hstl*
gruesome	*gr'sm*	heart	*hrt* or ♡	hot	*ht*
grumbler	*grmblr*	help	*hlp*	hot dog	*ht dg*
		her	*hr*	hothouse	*ht'hs*
		here	*hr*	hour	*hr.*

H

had	*hd*	hesitantly	*hztnt*	house	*hs*
hairpin	*hr'pn*	high	*he*	household	*hs'hld*
happily	*hp*	highway	*hiwa*	how	*hw*
hard	*hrd*	hill	*hl*	human	*hmn*
Harold	*Har.*	him	*hm*	humbly	*hmb*
Harry	*Har.*	himself	*hm'slf*	hunchbacked	*hnc'bk*

hundredfold	*hndrdfld*	induction	*ndkn*	it	*L*
huntsman	*hntsmn*	infirmary	*nfrmy*	italics	*ital.*
hurriedly	*hrd*	influence	*nflns*	its	*ts*
		information	*nfmn*	itself	*tslf*
		inquired	*nqr*		

I

icebox	*isbx*	insert	*1*	
ideas	*idz*	inside	*nsd*	
identities	*idntz*	inspection	*npn*	
if	*f*	inspiration	*npran*	

J

James	*Jas.*
January	*Jan.*
job	*jb*
July	*Jul.*

image	*mg*	instance	*nSns*	jumbled	*jmbl*
imaginary	*mgny*	instant	*nSnt*	June	*Jn* or *Ju.*
impertinent	*mprtnt*	instruction	*nStrcn*	junior	*jr.*
important	*mpnt* or *imp.*	intelligent	*ntlgt*	just	*jst*
impressive	*mprsv*	interesting	*ntg*	

K

improvement	*mprvt*	interrupt	*ntrpt*	
in	*n*	into	*∿*	kept	*kpt*
inch	*in.*	introduction	*intro.*	keyboard	*k'brd*
incision	*nsn*	inventive	*nvnv*	kind	*knd*
inclination	*nklnsn*	investigate	*nvstgt*	king	*kg*
increased	*nkrs*	invitation	*nvtan*	kitchen	*ktcn*
indent	*nt*	is	*s*	

knife	*knf*	lesson	*lsn*	lot	*lt*
know	*kn*	library	*lbry*	lovable	*lvl*
knowledge	*kndg*	life	*lf*	love	*lv*
		light	*lt*	loving	*lvg*
		lightheartedness	*lihrtdns*	lucky	*lky*
L		lighthouse	*lihs*		

laboratories	*lbrtz*	like	*lk*	**M**	
lacked	*lk—*	listened	*lsn—*		
ladder	*ldr*	listening	*lsng*	machine	*mSn*
lake	*lk*	little	*lil*	made	*md*
large	*lg*	live	*lv*	maid	*md*
late	*lt*	living	*lvg*	mailman	*ml'mn*
lately	*lly*	living room	*lvg rm*	maintaining	*mnlng*
laughing	*lfg*	loaned	*ln—*	major	*mzr*
lead	*ld*	locality	*lkll*	majority	*mjrt*
learn	*lrn*	location	*lkn*	make	*mk*
learning	*lrng*	lodestone	*ld'Sn*	man	*♂*
leave	*lv*	longer	*lngr*	manner	*mnr*
left	*lfl*	look	*lk*	many	*mny*
legible	*lgl*	loose	*ls*	March	*Mrc*
less and less	*(ls)*	lost	*lsl*	marching	*mrCg*
lesser	*lsr*			marked	*mrk—*

martyred	*mrtr*	mile	*ml*	mother	*mor*
Mary	*Ma.*	milk	*mlk*	mountain	*mt.*
masculine	*msc*	milkman	*mlk'mn*	mouse	*ms*
massive	*mv*	million	*mln* or 10^6	movable	*mvl*
master	*msr*	minus	*mn* or —	moved	*mvd*
masterful	*msrfl*	minute by minute	(*mnt*)	movement	*mvmt*
mate	*mt*	miscellaneous	*misc.*	mowed	*mw*
mathematics	*math.*	misery	*mzry*	much	*mC*
maturity	*mtrt*	mission	*mn*	multiply	X
may	*my*	mistake	*mstk*	must	*mst*
May	*My.*	mister	*mr.*	my	*m·*
maybe	*mab*	modern	*mdrn*	mystery	*mstry*
me	*m*	moment	*mmt*		
means	*mnz*	momentarily	*mmntr*	**N**	
meantime	*mn'tm*	Monday	*Mon.* or *M.*	narrative	*nrr*
measure	*mzr*	monetary	*mnty*	nation	*nn*
mechanics	*mknkz*	money	*mny* or $	nature	*nr*
medicine	*mdsn*	more	*mr*	necessary	*nssy*
meeting	*mtg*	more and more	(*mr*) or ⊕	necklace	*nk'ls*
memories	*mmrz*	mortality	*mrtlt*	need	*nd*
middle	*md*	most	*mst*	never	*vr*

Word	Sign	Word	Sign	Word	Sign
new	nu	occurred	okr	ounce	oz.
nice	ns	ocean	on	our	or
night	nt	October	Oct.	out	ot
no	no	odor	or	outside	o'sd
noisily	nz	of	f	outsider	o'sdr
none	nn	office	ofs	over	⌒
north	N	officer	ofsr	over and over	⌒⌒
northland	N'lnd	old	old	overcoat	O'kt
nosebleed	nz'bld	omit	omt	overdue	O'du
not	n	on	o	overestimate	o'stmt
nothing	ntg	once	/	overhang	O'hng
notion	nn	one	/	overhaul	O'hl
November	Nov.	only	⌒	overhead	O'hd
now	w	opera	opra	overlap	O'lp
number	#	or	or	overlook	O'lk
		orange	orng	overpass	O'ps
		order	ordr	overpower	O'pwr
O		organization	organzan	override	O'rd
oak	ok	originality	orgnlt	overseer	O'sr
oatmeal	ot'ml	originally	orgnly	overtime	O'tm
objective	objkv	other	otr	overtone	O'tn
occasionally	oksny				

overture	*O'tr*	people	*ppl*	pool	*pl*
overuse	*O'vz*	pepperbox	*ppr'bx*	poor	*pr*
overwork	*O'wrk*	percent	*%*	popcorn	*pp'krn*
own	*on*	perfect	*prfk*	population	*pop.*
		perfection	*prfkn*	portion	*prn*
P		performed	*prfrmd*	portraying	*prtray*
		period	*prd*	position	*pzn*
Pacific	*Pac.*	permanent	*prmnt*	possible	*psl*
padded	*pd*	persistence	*prsstns*	postcard	*p'skrd*
page	*p.*	person	*prsn*	potatoes	*pot.*
pages	*pp.*	picture	*pkr*	pound	*lb.*
painting	*pntg*	pieces	*psz*	power	*pwr*
paper	*ppr*	pillowcase	*plöks*	practiced	*prkts*
parallel	*‖*	place	*pls*	prejudice	*pryds*
part	*prt*	placement	*pls't*	preoccupy	*prekpr*
participating	*prtspt g*	played	*pld*	prerogative	*prgtv*
passable	*psl*	please	*plz*	present	*przt*
passive	*psv*	plus	*+*	president	*przdt*
past	*pst*	pneumonia	*nmna*	pressure	*prsr*
pattern	*ptrn*	pole	*pl*	primary	*prmy*
pavement	*pvt*	political	*pltkl*	printed	*prnt*
peace	*ps*				

problem	*prblm*
professor	*prof.*
progress	*prgrs*
promiscuity	*prmskt*
protect	*prtk*
protection	*prtkn*
providing	*prvdg*
Pullman	*Pl'mn*
purebred	*pr'brd*
purpose	*prps*

Q

quaint	*kwnt*
quality	*qval.*
queen	*kwn*
queer	*kwr*
question	*?*
quickly	*kwk*
quite	*kwt*
quotation	*kwtn*

R

race	*rs*
railroad	*rr.*
rain	*rn*
rainbow	*rn'bo*
raincoat	*rn'kt*
ran	*rn*
rapid-write	*rpd-rt*
reach	*rC*
reactive	*rkv*
read	*rd*
reader	*rdr*
reality	*rlt*
reason	*rzn*
recalling	*rklg*
receiving	*rsvg*
reducing	*rdsg*
reeling	*rlg*
reflection	*rflkn*
regarding	*rgdg*

relation	*rltn*
relative	*rlav*
released	*rls*
reliable	*rlbl*
reminded	*rmnd*
remove	*rmv*
rendezvous	*rndvu*
replies	*rplz*
research	*rsrC*
reside	*rzd*
resident	*rst*
resolved	*rzlv*
respectability	*rSktlt*
responsive	*rSnv*
rest	*rst*
restaurant	*rstrnt*
restrictive	*rSrkv*
restroom	*rS'm*
resulted	*rslt*
revolution	*rlrt*
Richard	*Rch. or Dick*

rigid	*rgd*	say	*sa*	shake	*sk*	
rimmed	*rm*	scarecrow	*skicro*	shallow	*slo*	
risking	*rskg*	school	*skl*	shame	*sm*	
river	*rvr*	scoutmaster	*sklmsr*	share	*sr*	
road	*rd.*	scrapbook	*skrpbk*	shave	*sv*	
room	*rm*	search	*src*	she	*se*	
root	*rt*	security	*skrt*	sheet	*st*	
row	*ro*	see	*se*	shell	*sl*	
rowboat	*robt*	seemed	*sem*	shelter	*sltr*	
rubber	*rbr*	senator	*snr*	shepherd	*sprd*	
running	*rng*	senior	*sr.*	sherbet	*srbt*	
rye	*ry*	sensation	*snsn*	shingle	*sngl*	
		sensible	*snsl*	shiver	*svr*	
S		sensory	*snsy*	shoestring	*S Srg*	
said	*sd*	September	*Sept.*	short	*srt*	
sailboat	*slbt*	servicewoman	*srvsmn*	should	*Sd*	
sandwich	*sndwc*	setback	*stbk*	shoulders	*sldrz*	
sat	*st*	setting	*stg*	shout	*st*	
Saturday	*Sat.*	sew	S	show	*so*	
save	*sv*	sewing	*Sg*	showed	*so*	
saw	*sw*	shadows	*Sdoz*	showing	*sog*	

sidewalk	*sd'wlk*	somewhere	*sm'we*	stadium	*Sdm*
sign	*sn*	son	*sn*	staggered	*Sgr*
silence	*slns*	soon	*sn*	staircase	*Sṙks*
simple	*smpl*	soul	*sl*	stairway	*Sṙwa*
since	*sns*	space	*Ps*	stalled	*Sl*
singing	*sgg*	sparse	*Prs*	stamp	*Smp*
sister	*ssr*	spartan	*Prtn*	standard	*Sndrd*
sit	*st*	special	*PSl*	starts	*Srtz*
situation	*stn*	spell	*Pl*	starve	*Srv*
skill	*skl*	spent	*Pnt*	state	*St*
slander	*slndr*	spider	*Pdr*	station	*San*
sleigh	*sla*	spinning	*Png*	stay	*Sa*
slippery	*slpy*	spirit	*Prt*	steel	*Sl*
slope	*slp*	spite	*Pt*	sterilize	*Srlz*
so	*S*	splash	*PlS*	stifle	*Sfl*
socially	*sS*	split	*Pll*	still	*Sl*
society	*sst*	spoil	*Pl*	stitch	*Stc*
some	*sm*	spoken	*Pkn*	stocking	*Skg*
something	*sm'ng*	spoon	*Pn*	stockpile	*Sk'pl*
sometimes	*sm'tmz*	spring	*Prg*	stoic	*Sok*
somewhat	*sm'wt*	square	□	stole	*Sol*

stone	*Son*	substance	*SSns*	tanned	*lan—*
stoneware	*Sonwr*	substitute	*SSlul*	tarry	*lry*
stood	*Sd*	suburban	*Srbn*	task	*lsk*
stop	*Sp*	success	*skss*	teach	*lC*
stoplight	*Sp'll*	successor	*skssr*	teacher	*lCr*
stopwatch	*Spwlc*	suit	*sl*	team	*lm*
store	*Sr*	summary	*smy*	tedious	*lds*
street	*Srl*	sun	*sn*	telegram	*llgrm*
struggle	*Srgl*	Sunday	*sndy* or *Su.*	telephone	*llfn*
study	*Sdy*	sunset	*sn'sl*	tell	*ll*
subject	*Sbyk*	sure	*Sr*	tenderhearted	*lndr'♡—*
subjective	*Sbyklv*	Susan	*Sue*	tension	*lnn*
subjunctive	*Sbynklv*	suspicion	*sbn*	tent	*lnl*
sublease	*Sls*	swinging	*sgg*	than	*ln*
sublet	*Sll*	swirling	*swrlg*	thanks	*lks*
sublimate	*Slml*			that	*tl*
sublime	*Slm*			the	**
submarine	*Smrn*	**T**		theater	*thr*
submission	*Smn*			theft	*tfl*
submit	*Sml*	tables	*lblz*	their	*tr*
subsidy	*Ssd*	taken	*lkn*	them	*tm*
		talented	*llnl—*		
		tame	*lm*		

theme	*tm*	threatened	*trtn—*	touch	*tc*	
themselves	*tm'slvz*	through	*tru*	toward	*twrd*	
theology	*tolgy*	throughout	*truot*	towboat	*tobt*	
theory	*try*	thunder	*tnr*	transformation	*trnsfrmn*	
there	*tr*	thunderbolt	*tnrblt*	treasurer	*trzrr*	
therefore	*∴*	Thursday	*thsdy*	treasury	*trzy*	
these	*tes*	thwart	*twrt*	tree	*tre*	
they	*ta*	tight	*tt*	try	*tru*	
thick	*tk*	time	*tm*	Tuesday	*tsdy*	
thin	*tn*	to	*2*	tumble	*tmbl*	
thing	*tg*	today	*2da*	turned	*trn—*	
think	*tnk*	tomato	*2mto*	turtleneck	*trtlnk*	
thirteen	*trtn*	tomorrow	*2moro*	tutor	*ttr*	
this	*ts*	tongue	*tng*	twenty	*20*	
Thomas	*tms*	too	*2*	twice	*2's*	
thorough	*tro*	took	*tk*	two	*2*	
those	*ths*	toothpaste	*ttps*			
though	*to*	topcoat	*tpkt*	**U**		
thought	*tt*	torture	*trtr*	ultramarine	*ultimrn*	
thread	*trd*	toss-up	*tsp*	ultranationalism	*ultrnnlsm*	

umbrella	*mbrla*	unfrosted	*nfrst*	very	*v*
unable	*unbl*	union	*unn*	view	*vv*
uncle	*uncl*	unless	*unls*	visible	*vzl*
under	*⌣*	up	*↑*	voice	*vs*
undercurrent	*U'krl*	upon	*upn*	vote	*vt*
underdog	*U'dg*	upper	*upr*		
underfoot	*U'ft*	upsetting	*up'stg*	**W**	
undergo	*U'go*	upstairs	*up'Srz*	wait	*wt*
underhanded	*U'hnd*	us	*vs*	waiting	*wtg*
underline	*U'ln*	uses	*usz*	walked	*wlk*
undermine	*U'mn*	useless	*vsls*	want	*wnt*
underneath	*U'nt*	usual	*vzl*	warily	*wr*
underpaid	*U'pd*	utility	*vlt*	warning	*wrng*
undersea	*U'se*			was	*z*
understanding	*U'Sndg*	**V**		washer	*wSr*
understudy	*U'Sdy*	vacuum	*vkm*	washes	*wSs*
undervalue	*U'vlv*	valley	*vl*	Washington	*Wash.*
underwater	*U'wtr*	value	*vlv*	watch	*wtC*
underwear	*U'wr*	vase	*vs*	water	*wtr*
underweight	*U'wt*	veal	*vl*	waterfall	*wtrfl*
unfortunate	*n4tn8*	vegetable	*veg.*	way	*wa*

we	*we*	wire	*wr*	would	*wld*
Wednesday	*Wed.* or *W.*	wired	*wrd*	wraiths	*rs*
week	*wk*	wisdom	*wzdm*	wringing	*rgg*
went	*we*	with	*w*	writers	*rrz*
were	*wr*	withal	*wl*	writing	*rn*
what	*we*	withdrawing	*W'drwg*	written	*rg*
when	*wn*	wither	*Wr*	wrote	*re*
where	*wr*	withhold	*W'hld*		
which	*wh*	within	*W'n*	**Y**	
while	*wl*	without	*W'ot*	yacht	*yt*
who	*hu*	withstand	*W'std*	yard	*yd.*
why	*why*	woman	*wmn* or ♀	year	*yr*
wildest	*wlds*	words	*wds*	year after year	⟨*yr*⟩
will	*wl*	wore	*wr*	yesterday	*ysr'da*
willingly	*wlg)*	work	*wk*	you	*U*
win	*wn*	world	*wrld*	your	*yr*
window	*wndw*	worry	*wry*		